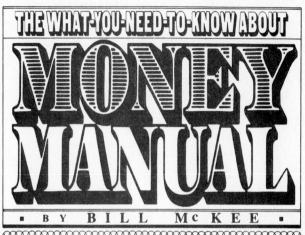

THE WHAT-YOU-NEED-TO-KNOW ABOUT MONEY MANUAL

• BY BILL McKEE •

SHELTER PUBLICATIONS, INC.
P.O. BOX 279, BOLINAS, CALIF. 94924

Shelter Publications, Inc.
P.O. Box 279
Bolinas, CA 94924

Copyright © 1989 Bill McKee

Distributed in the United States by:
TEN SPEED PRESS
P.O. Box 7123
Berkeley, California 94707

Library of Congress
Cataloging in Publication Data

McKee, Bill, 1935—
     The what-you-need-to-know about money manual / by Bill McKee.
          p.   cm.
     Bibliography: p.
     ISBN 0-89815-338-7 : $7.95
     1. Money—Dictionaries. 2. Finance—Dictionaries. I. Title.
HG216,M35 1989
332. 4'03—dc20   89-6417
                                                                     CIP

Additional copies of this book may be purchased for
$7.95 plus $2.00 shipping/handling1st book, 75¢ each
additional book from Shelter Publications, Inc.

CONTENTS

MONEY DUMB

Over the years, my personal money management has been dumb.

Careless use of credit cards and installment buying. Cars and houses bought because of low monthly payments, with no thought to finance costs. Selling a house in a buyer's market, instead of renting it and waiting for a better price. Making money in commodities without knowing why or how. Spending dividends frivolously. Name a wrong move, and I made it.

Then came the capper: advising my daughters to buy a mutual fund from an old friend. With none of us — daughters, dad nor friend — knowing the difference between a high risk fund and a conservative one or even whether it was a good time to buy any fund. It wasn't. And daughters no longer ask dad's advice.

The bottom line, as the money folks say, was that my financial skills needed work. A beginner's guide seemed the right place to start, but I couldn't find one. So I started digging — through stocks, bonds, commodities, all of it — and what I learned became *The Money Manual*. You might say it's the by-product of a two year journey from moneydumb to moneysmart(er).

> *"Money was made for the free-hearted and generous."*
> *John Gay*

WHAT THE
MONEY MANUAL
IS NOT

No financial advice or recommendations are presented in
The Money Manual: your money decisions are your own. Nor
is this a how-to-get-rich-quick book. If we knew that secret,
the price of this book would be considerably more than what
you paid. We agree with Kin Hubbard who said: "The fastest
way to double your money is to fold it in half and put it in
your pocket."

WHAT IT IS

Bulls and bears, deflation and inflation, commodities, mutual
funds, GNP, LBO, going public: all are money words you'll
find in your morning paper. And when you compare today's
paper with one from ten years ago, the increase in financial
subjects and coverage is staggering.

The subjects are critical ones. As health and other
insurance costs go out of sight, as social security and support
systems we once relied on get shaky, as taxes take a bigger
and bigger bite, money becomes a subject you and I *must*
understand.

But just as transmission specialists and eye doctors have
professional methods and vocabularies, so do bankers, tax
auditors and commodity traders. The amateur needs to know
enough of their language to successfully interface with the pros.
The Money Manual helps smooth that interface.

AND HOW TO USE IT

1. For an overview, browse pages 10 through 24. The nine money sections starting on page 14 are a helpful background for the material that follows.

2. For a particular word or phrase see "Moneytalk A to Z" (pages 25 to 200); examples illustrate many entries. Definitions are alphabetized, but also may appear under major related listings: "Stock Market" under "Stock," "Life Insurance" under "Insurance," and so on. General subjects — banks, mortgages, taxes, etc., are also covered in detail.

3. Sections on "Money Slang," "Some Other People's Money," "Money Media" and "Money Initials" complete the volume.

The Money Manual is a book-full, but we've tried to keep it simple and entertaining as well as informative. Comments, feedback and suggestions are welcomed and will be considered in future editions. §

"A rich man and his daughter are soon parted."
Kin Hubbard

SAVING
LOW RISK

When you put cash in a savings account with a sound bank, you're almost certain to get your money back, plus interest earned. Some people think of that cash as invested, but it's so risk-free and the income is so predictable that it classifies as savings, pure and simple.

> **Characteristics:** Low-risk, very liquid, little time and money management skill required. Low returns.

Investment
MEDIUM RISK

A stock with a track record for reasonable performance will be a higher risk than the savings account; it also offers the potential for greater rewards. If you invest in stock, bonds, real estate, etc., you hope to get your cash back — plus. But you accept extra risk for the potential of extra reward.

> **Characteristics:** Medium to high risk, liquid, time and money management skill required. Potential for medium to high returns.

SPECULATION
HIGH RISK

Some say there's little difference between investment and speculation. But if you put cash into something of such high risk as to have double-or-nothing potential (such as a highly leveraged commodities account or a wildcat oil exploration), you are definitely in the gambler's realm of speculation.

> **Characteristics:** High risk, may not be liquid; time and money management skill required. Potential for large gains — and equally large losses. $

L I Q U I D I T Y

If you invest your cash, you don't want it hopelessly tied up: if you need it back, you want to get it quickly, without penalty. A savings or investment plan that offers this feature is said to be *liquid*, it has *liquidity*.

Liquidity simply means having a customer available for what you want to sell, when you want to sell it. (Liquidity is often confused with marketability; stocks, bonds, and commodities are liquid — there's always a ready market for them. *But* the price the market offers may be very unattractive.)

For each of the nine categories that follow, liquidity is rated by the author (page 24) for comparison.

RISK

The higher an investment's potential for big gains, the greater the risk, i.e., potential for big losses. Logical, isn't it? And fair.

Each of us has an investment risk tolerance level. (There are even tolerance tests for would-be investors.)

Be aware of your risk tolerance. If an investment keeps you awake nights it's probably time to consider investing at a lower risk level. (See risk ratings on page 24.) $

interest & INFLATION

Times are good. Jobs are plentiful, wages rising. People are optimistic, spending money, borrowing to buy what they want.

Then things get out of hand. Consumer demand gets too strong, there's too much spending, too much borrowing. Prices go up, our money buys less, is worth less. Suddenly, we've got *inflation*.

Now our exports get more expensive and the balance of trade takes a beating; jobs are lost, there's no demand and, and, and . . .

So the FED steps in, hikes the interest rate — which makes purchases even more expensive for a while. But higher rates eventually discourage spending and encourage saving. And inflation slows.

Government uses the interest rate to warm or cool the economy. When you hear on the news that the FED has raised the *prime interest rate*, you know:

- mortgage rates will go up, real estate sales slow down;
- you'll pay higher interest for your new car loan, but your savings should also earn a higher rate;
- business costs will go up (which results in higher prices which reduces sales which lowers corporate profits) so your stocks' value may drop;
- bond prices will also drop as better interest rates become available elsewhere. Investment accounts suffer as scared money moves to the security of interest-bearing accounts, on which the rates are rising.

That's greatly oversimplified, but you get the idea. So what can you and I do about it all? Not much. Just be aware of it when making spending, saving, and business plans and act accordingly. The chart on page 24 shows how money responds to interest and inflation. $

MONEY & Age

Age is a key factor in wise money management.

For example: a 30-year-old with a good income and no responsibilities may have no interest in life insurance. Real estate, stocks and other investments may be more appealing — even some aggressive high risk investments. If they hit, it's a big head-start. But if they go sour, a young person has time to recover from the loss.

A 45-year-old may have a higher income than the younger person, but also have a big mortgage, kids to send to college: responsibilities. Life insurance is a must and a more cautious, balanced investment program is in order, since death or a large financial loss could destroy the entire family's lifestyle and future.

Now consider a 60-year old with house paid off, the kids grown up and a comfortable retirement a few years down the road. Such a person would probably invest conservatively because at this point in life there's little time left to recover from a large loss. §

Savings and investments for the three might look like this:

	AGE 30 *growing income*	AGE 45 *peak income*	AGE 60 *static income*
Savings	20%	25%	50%
Investments			
Conservative low risk	20%	40%	40%
Average medium risk	40%	30%	10%
Aggressive high risk	20%	5%	0%

This example also illustrates the strategy of putting financial eggs into several baskets.

MONEY
HOW A DOLLAR IS PUT TOGETHER

1.
CASH

2.
SAVING

3.
INSURANCE

4.
REAL
ESTATE

5.
COLLECTIBLE

6.
MUTUAL
FUND

7.
STOCK

8.
BOND

9.
COMMODITY

&
MORE . . .

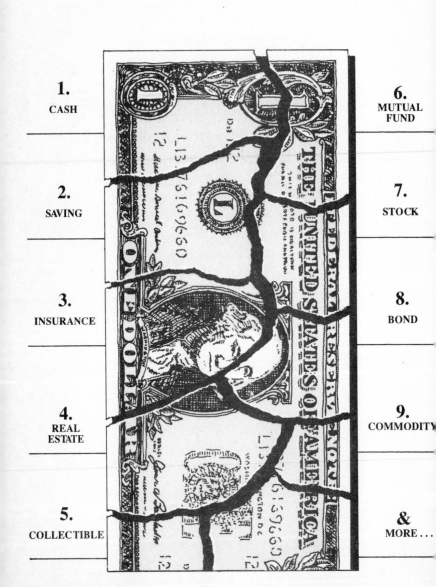

Webster says money is:
*"Something generally accepted
as a medium of exchange, a means of payment,
a measure of value."*
This is a broad definition — even more broadly interpreted
here to include personal assets in the following
nine categories.

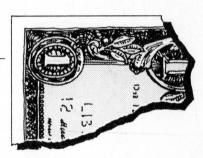

1. CASH

Coins
Currency
Checking Accounts

Say money and most of us think cash. You could call cash *running money*, because without bills, coins or a check in your pocket, you'd be hard pressed to get through the day.

As you can spend it at any time, cash has the ultimate liquidity. It's safe, too, without risk — so long as your pocket is free of holes and your bank is solvent. 💲

SEE THESE CASH–RELATED ALPHABETICAL LISTINGS:
Average Daily Balance; Bank; Barter; Cashier's Check; Checking Account; Credit; Currency; Demand; Exchange Rate; Fiat Money; Inflation; Joint Account; Liquidity; Overdraft; Service Charge.

2. SAVINGS

Passbook
Money Markets
CDs
T-Bills, etc.

Saving: *delayed gratification,* laying money away in order to comfortably afford something later — instead of uncomfortably buying the something right now.

Lend the money you save to a bank, a Savings & Loan or the government, and they will pay you interest for the use of it.

Such savings are liquid: you can get your hands on your cash if you need it. It's safe and risk-free, provided the institution you choose is sound.

And saving is smart: you get security against a rainy day, while using your cash to earn more. $

SEE THESE SAVINGS–RELATED ALPHABETICAL LISTINGS:
Accounts (CD; Interest Bearing; Passbook; Joint); Credit Union; Early Withdrawal Penalty; Interest (Compound; Simple, Prime), Money Market; Pension; Principal; Retirement Plans (KEOGH; IRA; SEPP); Risk; Save; S&L; Social Security; Treasury (Certificates; Savings Bond; T-Bill; T-Bond); Time Deposit.

3. INSURANCE —————

The world is a jungle filled with bad things waiting to happen. Life, health, car, house, business, whatever, are always at risk.

Odds are your house won't burn down. *But* if the possibility worries you and you couldn't afford to replace the house, you can share the risk — by buying insurance.

As well as insuring risk, some *life* insurance policies offer equity-building features with savings and tax benefits.

Insurance comes in all shapes and sizes. The trick is to have enough of the right kind for your personal situation, without being insurance-poor. $

UNDER INSURANCE, SEE THESE LISTINGS:

Agent; Policies (Accident, Automobile, Business, Casualty, Disability, Group, Liability, Mortgage, Life — Annuity, Decreasing Term, Endowment, Ordinary Life, Single-Premium, Straight Life, Whole Life, Convertible, Double-Indemnity); Policy Deductible; Policyholder; Policy Loan (Cash Value; Loan Value); Policy Premium; Waiver of Premium; Short-rate; Policy Rider; Policy Surrender.

SEE ALSO: *Estate; Tax; Trustee.*

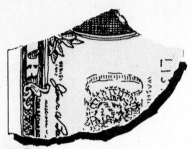

4. REAL ESTATE

Most money things are intangible. Sure, you can see and feel a dollar bill, but the bill itself is a useless piece of paper.

Real estate is tangible — a *real* thing (it's a *hard asset,* as are collectibles and commodities). You can see and feel and use a house. And, like cash, it has value.

Real estate, however, has different risk and liquidity considerations than cash: should you want to sell, finding a customer who will pay your price when you want it may not be so easy. §

UNDER REAL ESTATE, SEE THESE LISTINGS:

Closing; Closing Costs; Types of Real Estate (Apartment; Condominium; Co-op; Commercial Real Estate; Income Property; Land; Residence; Second Home; Timeshare; Shopping Center); Realtor.

SEE ALSO: *Depreciation; Estate; Interest; Lease; Mortgage; Insurance; Rent; Title.*

5. COLLECTIBLES

Baseball cards or Picassos, most of us have collections. But not necessarily collections of collectibles.

When rarity, beauty and/or uniqueness lend an item desirability (value) beyond utility, the item becomes a collectible.

A professional art or antique dealer can earn a nice living trading collectibles. The pros advise amateurs to buy for enjoyment and pleasure — if you get a good investment as well, lucky you.

Like real estate, a collectible is tangible and to sell it you must find a customer: a liquidity problem. And collectible pricing is subjective, what the market will bear, so there is risk (a big risk, if you bought at a premium). 💲

UNDER COLLECTIBLES, SEE THESE LISTINGS:
Antiques; Coins; Gems; Oriental Rugs; Stamps; Art.

6. STOCK

In order to raise cash to start up or expand, a business may divide its value (equity) into parts and sell some of those parts.

The parts are called stock — just as the extra cans of soup in the back room of the corner grocery are parts of the business and are called stock.

Depending on the business' structure, stock may be offered privately — to management, employees, etc. — or it may be sold to the public. If you buy stock, you own a piece of the business and you share in its success or lack of success.

The stock market provides assurance that there are always buyers for publicly traded stocks: high liquidity. But stock value can be volatile, so with ownership comes risks.

The SEC — Securities and Exchange Commission — oversees and regulates the trading of stocks and bonds to help insure that investors get fair treatment. §

UNDER STOCK, SEE THESE LISTINGS:
Common Stock; Convertible Stock; Preferred Stock; Stockbroker; Stock Certificate; Stock Company; Stock Exchange; Stockholder; Stockholders' Equity; Stock Index; Stock Ledger; Stock Market; Stock Option; Stock Offer; Stock Split; Stock Symbol; Unbundled Stock.

SEE ALSO: *Averaging; Balanced Portfolio; Blue Chip; Broker; Business Structures; Buy and Hold; Commission; Dividends; Dow-Jones; Earnings; Index; Insider Trading; Investment; Margin; Option; SEC.*

7. BONDS

Bonds are used by business and government to borrow for big, long-term projects. (Bonds are *debt instruments* — I.O.U.s. Unlike stocks, bonds don't represent equity in the business or institution that issues them.)

Example: to build a new subway, a city government floats (offers) a $10 million issue of 7%, 30-year municipal bonds.

Translation: you can lend as much as $10 million to the city, for which it will give you bonds that pay 7% annual interest for the next 30 years. Then the city will redeem (buy back) its bonds from you at their face value.

Sound like sure income? It is, maybe even tax-free.

Of course, interest rates may go up from what your bonds pay, so the deal may not stay as sweet as it starts out. Then the bonds' face value may drop below what you paid. And if rates go up, the bond issuer may be able to redeem your bonds before maturity. Those are the risks.

Liquidity is average, but varies depending on whether the issue is large or small, municipal or corporate, the quality rating high or low. The secondary bond market provides ready customers when you decide to sell (but selling before maturity can be an expensive proposition). $

UNDER BONDS, SEE THESE LISTINGS:

SEE ALSO: *Treasury*

8. MUTUAL FUNDS

Q. With capital, some knowledge and willingness to accept risk, what more does the would-be investor need?

A. *Experience.* And the only way to get it is to play the game.

Buying shares in a mutual fund (also called simply a *fund*) is one way to get your feet wet.

A mutual fund is a company that invests in other businesses. It sells its own shares to other investors, pools the money and reinvests it.

Shareholder benefits are *diversification,* which reduces risk, and *lower trading costs* because of volume trading discounts. Perhaps the major benefit is *money management by a professional* — who may earn better results than most amateurs would get for themselves.

A fund may charge a fee (load) for its investment services and all funds charge management fees; investors must be sure to read the prospectus to know exactly what they are buying — and paying.

Liquidity is not a problem; funds are obligated to buy back their own shares. Funds range from ultra-conservative to extremely high risk.

The popularity with IRA and other pension plans is one reason funds have multiplied from a couple of hundred a few years ago to the thousands you can choose from today. $

UNDER MUTUAL FUND, SEE THESE LISTINGS:

Family of Funds; Load Funds; Telephone Switch; Types of Funds: Bond; Cash Reserves; Growth; Growth/Income; Income; Overseas; Sector.

SEE ALSO: *Commission; Retirement Plan; Tax.*

9. COMMODITIES

Certain useful goods, such as wheat, corn, cattle, lumber and oil, are commodities bought and sold on the commodity markets.

There are straightforward cash markets — and there are *futures markets.* (The commodities are to be delivered in the future: the market may exist before the commodities do.)

The futures markets work like this: trading units — 1000 ounces of silver, 5000 bushels of wheat, etc. — are called contracts, and are traded on margin: a percentage of total value. For margin money, a contract buyer/seller does not own the commodity: he owns the *right* to buy (or sell) the amount of the commodity contracted for, at the contract price, on the contracted future date.

Sound complicated? It is! Skill, large amounts of money, and nerves of steel are trading prerequisites. Because fortunes are made and lost overnight, money pros accurately call commodity trading *hardball.* The commodity market provides liquidity, but volatility and *high* risk make commodity trading pure speculation. **$**

UNDER COMMODITY, SEE THESE LISTINGS:
Commodity Exchange; Commodity Futures Contract; Commodity Futures Trading; Commodity (Futures) Trader.

SEE ALSO: *Hedging: Long/Short Position: Margin; Metals; Option; Speculation.*

AND BE SURE TO CHECK THESE OTHER IMPORTANT LISTINGS:
Bank; Business Structures; Interest; Mortgage; Retirement Plan; Tax; Treasury. Many other business, economic and finance entries also are defined, listed alphabetically.

RISK, LIQUIDITY, VALUE COMPARISON

	Risk	Liquidity	Value As Inflation Rises	Value As Interest Rises
CASH	Low	High	Drops	—
SAVINGS	Low	High	Drops	Rises
INSURANCE *(Life/equity)*	Low	Low	Drops[2]	Drops[2]
REAL ESTATE	Varies[1]	Varies[1]	Rises[4]	Drops[3]
COLLECTIBLES	High	Low	Rises[4]	Drops[3 & 4]
STOCKS	Varies[1]	Medium	Varies[1]	Varies[1]
BONDS	Varies[1]	Medium	Drops	Drops[3]
MUTUAL FUNDS	Varies[1]	Medium	Varies[1]	Varies[1]
COMMODITIES	High	Medium	Rises[4]	Varies[1 & 4]

1) *Depends on type: a) stock varies by company and industry, b) bonds vary dependent upon whether government, corporate, tax-free, and the quality ratings: c) real estate varies, whether residential or commercial.*

2) *Only cash values of equity-building life insurance policies are considered.*

3) *Investments and speculations usually move opposite to interest rates. When rates go up, business costs and, thus, product prices go up — which reduces sales and corporate profits. So securities may become less attractive, and investors may move their money into interest-bearing accounts for a low risk, higher rate of return.*

4) *The value of tangibles — collectibles, commodities, real estate — usually goes up when inflation rises.*

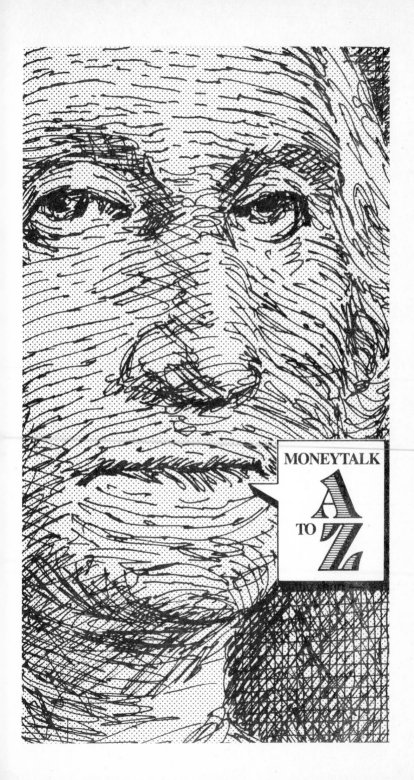

MONEYTALK
A
TO
Z

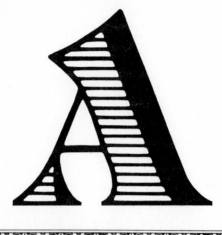

Abstract of Title   See: TITLE

Accelerated Depreciation   See: DEPRECIATION

Accident Insurance   See: INSURANCE

....

Account

Accounting/bookkeeping: A financial data record of asset, liability, income, expense and net worth items.

Client Account: Recorded personal, property or business transactions.   See also: BANK

....

Account Executive

Representative — of a brokerage, bank, advertising agency, etc.— who sells, services and manages customer accounts. Also called a *customers' man/woman/person*.

....

Accounting

The calculation and recording of financial accounts.

Accountant

One who does accounting — keeps, inspects and adjusts accounts.

CPA

Abbr. : **Certified Public Accountant**. To earn certification and a license, an accountant must have a degree in the field, serve an apprenticeship under a CPA and pass qualifying examinations. CPAs may do tax work, as well as accounting.

Accountants' Opinion

An opinion of the financial audit results a business reports, and of the accounting procedures used to arrive at those results.

Account Book

Book(s) where accounts are documented. May be an electronic (computer) documentation.

Accounting Firm

A group of accountants (usually CPAs); often the firm provides services required by large clients.

....

Account Number

Customer identification number for an account with a bank, store, brokerage, etc. In a literal sense, Social Security and federal identification numbers are also account numbers. *Numbered account:* for the sake of privacy (some say secrecy) Swiss banks identify customer accounts by number only. Also called a *Swiss account.*

....

Accounts Payable

Unsettled accounts a buyer (of goods/services) owes: accounts (liabilities) outstanding to be paid by a business. Also called *payables.*

....

Accounts Receivable

Unsettled accounts of a seller; accounts awaiting payment; obligations due from customers which represent business assets. Also called *receivables*.

Accrual (Method)

An accounting system in which receipts and payments are recorded as the transactions take place, instead of when cash is actually received or paid. Also called *accrual basis*. See also: CASH METHOD

Accrued Interest   See: INTEREST

Acquisition

A company acquired through purchase or takeover.

Actuarial Tables   See: INSURANCE

Adjustable Rate Mortgage   See: MORTGAGE

Administrator

A person or bank appointed by the courts to administer and distribute the estate of a deceased who left no will (or who left a will that names no executor).

AFL-CIO   See: UNION

Aggressive Growth Fund   See: MUTUAL FUND

Agribusiness

All-inclusive word referring to farming and related businesses for growing, marketing, processing, serving and supplying agriculture.

Amortize

To write off the cost of an asset over a period of time;
to liquidate an obligation, esp. by periodic payments.
Amortization: the act; also the amount. See also:
DEPRECIATION, TAX

Analyst   See: INVESTMENT ANALYST

Annual Meeting

One of a corporation's yearly management meetings, usually
held after the fiscal year has ended and financial results are
in. It's the meeting shareholders are most likely to attend,
at which they can vote on corporate matters, election of
the directors, etc. See also: CORPORATION, PROXY

Annual Report

The printed report furnished
to a company's stockholders
after the business year has
ended (usually at the time
of the annual meeting) which
summarizes the company's
previous year's financial
performance, market situation,
future plans, etc. It includes
charts of the financial results
and the accountants' opinion
of how results were arrived at.
The annual report is also a
public relations device used
to attract new investors, and
important to read before
investing in a company. See also:
QUARTERLY REPORT, ACCOUNTANTS' OPINION

"A billion dollars isn't what it used to be."
Nelson Bunker Hunt

Annuity See: INSURANCE

Antiques See: COLLECTIBLES

....

Antitrust

Federal laws against trusts or other combinations of businesses that might monopolize a market and restrain free trade. See also: TRUST, MONOPOLY

....

Apartment See: REAL ESTATE

APR See: INTEREST

....

Arbitrage

The buying of commodities, currencies, etc. on one market to sell at a higher price on another market, thus taking advantage of brief price discrepancies between the two markets for a profit.

Risk Arbitrage is arbitrage involving high risk, such as buying the stock of a company targeted for takeover (expecting its stock to rise), while at the same time selling the stock of the company making the takeover (expecting its stock to drop). While the profit potential is huge, so is the potential for loss — if the takeover falls through. A trader who practices arbitrage is called an *arbitrageur*. See also: HEDGING

....

Arrears

Unpaid bills, overdue debts. If you're two months behind in the rent, you're *in arrears*.

....

> *"Money won't buy happiness,
> but it will pay the salaries
> of a large research staff
> to study the problem."*
> *Bill Vaughan*

Asked Price (Bid Price)

The price asked by a seller; phrase implies a lower price might be accepted after bargaining. *Bid Price* is the price offered by a would-be buyer. See also: COMMODITIES, OPTIONS

Asset

Anything owned that has a cash or exchange value. A person's (or a business') cash, property, accounts receivable; property usable to pay debts. *Accounting:* assets minus liabilities show net worth. See also: LIABILITY

Fixed Asset

A business' permanent tangible assets: buildings, land, machinery, etc. that are not consumed or converted to cash in the course of doing business. Also called a *capital asset.*

Assess, Assessed Valuation, Assessment, Assessor   See: TAX
Assumable Mortgage   See: MORTGAGE

Auction

The sale of goods or property to the highest bidder.

Average Daily Balance

The sum of an account's daily balances for an accounting
period, divided by the number of days in the period.
Often refers to bank accounts; a service charge may be
imposed if a specified minimum average daily account
balance isn't maintained.

Averaging

Dollar (cost) averaging is an investment buying strategy:
buying a fixed dollar amount of securities, regardless of
price, at set time intervals. In the long run, this results in
an average purchase price higher than the security's lowest
selling price, but lower than its highest price. Averaging
assumes a long-term upward market trend.

> *"I'd like to be rich enough
> so I could throw soap away
> after the letters are worn off."*
> **Andy Rooney**

JACKSON

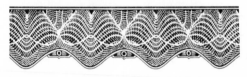

Balance of Trade

A nation's exports minus its imports. A plus result is a *positive balance of trade*; a minus is a *negative balance*.

Balance of Payments

Money owed by or due to a nation — resulting from the *balance of trade*.

....

Balance Sheet

A financial picture of a business at one point in time; a financial statement that itemizes assets and liabilities to determine net worth. Assets equal (balance with) liabilities plus net worth.

....

Balanced Portfolio

A group (portfolio) of several types of investments with different levels of risk, selected to maximize profit potential while minimizing risk. See also: PORTFOLIO, and the AGE & MONEY section

....

Balloon Payment

Portions of payments due (on a mortgage or loan) are
delayed until a later time when the deferred portions are
to be paid in one lump sum — called a *balloon payment*.
Popular during periods of high mortgage interest rates.
Caution — balloons burst. See also: MORTGAGE, VARIABLE
RATE INTEREST

> *"Money is just something to make
> bookkeeping convenient."*
> H.L. Hunt

► Bank

A business (federal/state chartered) that receives, keeps,
lends (customers) money and simplifies the exchange of
funds by handling checks, notes, etc. On savings deposits
and some other accounts, banks pay interest; for services,
eg., checking, credit cards, etc., they may charge fees.

A bank lends customers' funds to borrowers at a higher
interest rate than it pays depositors and, after expenses,
profits by the difference.

Banks, savings and loans, and brokerage houses formerly
provided separate and distinct financial services. With
deregulation and changes in the law, however, the dis-
tinctions between the institutions — and their services
— have blurred.

Bank Holiday

When a bank's obligations are greater than its resources, it may be forced to close the doors to customers while the problem is being resolved: a (forced) bank holiday.

Bankers' Hours

A short day. Banks traditionally are open to customers only from 10 a.m. to 3 p.m. Now, however, many banks are extending customer hours.

● TYPES OF BANKS

Central Bank: A nation's government bank — such as the *FED* — that sets and controls national financial policy and lends money to private financial institutions. See also: FED

Commercial Bank: Specializes in checking accounts and short-term loans. Commercial banks are the ones most of us use day-to-day.

Federal Reserve Bank: See: FEDERAL RESERVE SYSTEM

Full Service Bank: Offers a complete range of services, both lending and investment.

Investment Bank: Primary business is underwriting new securities. See also: UNDERWRITE

Merchant Bank: A private bank that invests primarily in new securities issues and in accepting bills of exchange in foreign trade.

Postal Savings Bank: Banks formerly operated by local post offices for small accounts.

Reserve Bank: One of the 12 principal banks of the U.S. Federal Reserve System; a bank authorized by a government to hold other banks' reserves. See also: FEDERAL RESERVE SYSTEM

Savings Bank: A bank that handles only savings accounts, paying interest on the accounts to depositors.

State Bank: A state chartered bank operating under that state's banking laws.

....

Bankruptcy

A business (or person) with more liabilities than assets may request protection from creditors while reorganizing; in the attempt to operate profitably, it voluntarily *files for bankruptcy.* (Creditors may also throw such a business into *involuntary* bankruptcy.) Chapters 7 or 11 of the legal code are commonly used, depending on the circumstances.

....

Barter

Instead of paying cash for goods or services, payment is made (bartered, traded) for other goods or services. Barter, the oldest method of payment, is regaining popularity; there are even organizations that broker barter deals. Be aware that the IRS keeps a sharp eye on the barter business.

....

BBB

Abbr.: **Better Business Bureau**. A national organization of businesses that establishes and polices guidelines and standards for ethical business practice among its members. The BBB has national and state organizations, with offices or representatives in most cities.

Consumers who think they have been unfairly treated by a business can take their complaints to the BBB. The Bureau will check the business for prior grievances and — if the complaint is valid — pressure the offender to satisfy the customer. The BBB also provides a number of other consumer services.

....

Bear

One who is pessimistic about the possibility for early gains (in the economy or a market) is said to be a bear. Of course, consistent losses can turn even the most optimistic investor (*a bull*) into a bear. *Bearish* refers to a bear's conservative attitude. *Bear Market:* investors as a group are bearish, due to a general downtrend in the markets. See also: BULL

"Bulls make money, bears make money, but pigs seldom do."
Wall Street Maxim

Bid Price   See: ASKED PRICE

Big Board

The moving electronic display found in the stock exchange(s) that indicates companies' shares listed and traded, and the prices. Also the *New York Stock Exchange* is sometimes called the big board.

Black Friday

On September 24, 1869, a group tried to corner the gold market and caused a panic that resulted in a depression: the first Black Friday. There have been others since. Now, a severe market drop may earn the Black Friday label on any day, be it Friday or Tuesday.

Black Monday

Monday, October 19, 1987, when the U.S. stock market dropped more than 500 points. See also: BLACK FRIDAY, SILVER THURSDAY

....

Blip

A movement, up or down, in a financial market which occurs for no apparent reason and doesn't relate to the market's overall direction.

....

Block

A large amount of a single security. Big investors such as institutions, pension funds, etc., trade in blocks. And big up/down swings in market prices often reflect active block trading. See also: INSTITUTIONAL BUYING/SELLING, PROGRAMMED TRADING

....

Blue Chip

Stock in companies (usually large) with a history (usually long) of positive financial performance and of paying regular dividends.
Also: a *Blue Chip Company*.

....

Board (of Directors)

Corporations have directors who appoint senior management, issue additional shares, set policy and plans, and are supposed to represent the stockholders' best interests. As they are insiders, how they trade their own stock in the

> *"When money speaks, the truth is silent."*
> **Russian Proverb**

corporation is restricted. Collectively, directors are called
the Board of Directors.

Directors may be drawn from a combination of: the
company's senior executives (*inside directors*); persons
outside the corporation (*outside directors*) whose fields
may relate to, or be important to, the company's business;
persons who own or represent the ownership of large
amounts of stock. See also: BUSINESS STRUCTURE,
CORPORATION, PROXY

Board Meeting

Periodic (usually quarterly) meetings of a company's
board of directors. See also: ANNUAL MEETING,
QUARTERLY MEETING

....

Boilerroom Operation

Where *unethical* sales people use high-pressure techniques
to sell securities over the phone. The talk is fast, the
manner intimidating, the rationale a loose interpretation
of fact combined with implied insider knowledge. The
products are invariably speculative, high-risk securities of
perhaps no value at all. And commissions are extreme, as
much as 25–30%.

....

▶ Bond

For large, long-term borrowings for big projects, such
as plant expansion, companies and governments issue
bonds: interest bearing certificates that can be redeemed
at a specified later date. While stock represents ownership
of a part of the issuing company, bonds do not: they only
represent debt. Bond liquidity is high; risk varies, dependent on the issuer, the bond type and the rating. Also
to bond: to secure an obligation by bond.

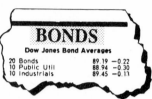

This is the first of several example tables and charts which appear daily on the financial pages of major newspapers. Presentation varies from paper to paper, but the data is the same — it all comes from the same computer.

Bonds have face values of $1000; the numbers shown are percentages so the price averages here are about $890. The last number is the change from the previous quote.

Bond Ratings

Quality ratings assigned to bonds by recognized rating services. AAA (unlikely to default) is the highest rating, D (in default) is lowest. Obviously the more 'A's, the more attractive a bond is to investors.

High-Grade Bonds

Superior quality, highly rated (AAA, AA) Bonds.

● TYPES OF BONDS

Agency Bond: Issued by a government agency (such as the Federal National Mortgage Association — Fannie Mae).

Baby Bond: Has less than $1,000 (par) value.

Convertible Bond: Can be exchanged for shares of the issuing company's common stock, at the bond holder's option. The company can also force conversion.

Corporate Bond: Issued to raise money for a private corporation.

Coupon Bond: A bond with detachable coupons that must be presented to the issuer to get interest earned. *Registered bonds* pay interest without coupons and are replacing the older coupon variety.

Discount Bond: Sold at a price lower than face value, which makes it more attractive to buyers during times when market interest rates are higher than the rate the bond pays.

General Obligation Bond: Issued by a state or city, backed by general tax revenue and the issuer's credit. See also: REVENUE BOND

Government Bond: See: TREASURY

> *"Gentlemen prefer bonds."*
> *Andrew Mellon*

Junk Bond: High-yield bonds, usually low-rated because of questionable value and often sold at a discount. Called *junk* because of the high debt levels of the issuing companies. They're considered speculative, very high risk; a device often used to generate takeover money for leveraged buyouts. See also: LBO, TAKEOVER

Municipal Bond (MUNIS): Issued by a state, county, town, city or by a state agency to finance public projects.

Revenue Bond: Issued to finance a specific project; the income generated is used to repay the bond. Ex.: a municipal bond for a sewer system.

Savings Bond See: TREASURY

Tax-Free Bond: Classes of bonds issued by governments which are not subject to certain taxes (ex.: state tax). Depending on the investors' tax bracket, the tax-free feature may provide a higher yield, which makes the bonds attractive.

Zero-Coupon Bond: A debt obligation (bond) that pays no interest, but that sells well below its ultimate redeemable face value. (There are no coupons; they're clipped off.) These bonds appreciate each year.

Bond Fund: See: MUTUAL FUND

Book

In a stock brokerage, a group of related stocks (managed by one person or group) is a book. See also: PORTFOLIO

Book Entry

A securities transaction with no deliverable certificate: the customer gets only statements (from his broker).

Books (The)

Accounting records, ledgers of a business.

Book Value

The intrinsic value price of a stock or bond, arrived at by dividing net worth of the issuing organization by total shares outstanding.

Bottom Line

Net income or profit from business performance; the end result (of an action).

Bourse

European stock exchanges.

Breakout

A sudden price increase of a security or commodity.

Broker

Insurance, mortgage, real estate, securities, etc.: One who represents another to buy or sell property, products, services. For his work the broker earns a commission, a percentage of the deal brokered.

Brokers represent more than one seller. (An agent represents one seller, exclusively.) Also: to negotiate, to act as middleman.

> *"Brokee: Someone who buys stock on the advice of a broker."*
> *Jim Fisk & Robert Barron*

Brokerage (House, Firm)

An organization or group offering broker services. Also: the *business* and *commission* of a *broker*.

Discount Brokerage

Charges lower than traditional commissions. Services — research, etc.— available from *full-service brokerages* aren't offered, but knowledgeable traders who do their own research find the discount prices most attractive.

Budget

An itemized estimate of income and expenses for a stated period of time in the future.

Budget Deficit: The amount by which out-go exceeds income. Lower income or higher costs (or a combination) than budgeted for results in a deficit.

....

Bull

An investor optimistic about future gains in the economy or a market is called a bull (opposite of bear). *Bullish:* an optimistic attitude. A market consistently going up is a *bull market*. See also: BEAR

....

Bullion

Gold or silver in the form of bars or ingots.
See also: METALS

....

Business Cycle   See: CYCLES

....

▶ BUSINESS STRUCTURES

● Company

A group united for joint action, esp. business.

Limited Company (Ltd.)

A European and Canadian structure: shareholder responsibility for company debt is limited to the amount they invest in the company.

Private Company

A company where shares are owned by management, employees, family, but aren't sold to the public. Also called a *closely-held* company.

Public Company

A company whose shares are sold to the public. Public company shares and procedures are regulated by the SEC. Also called a *publicly-held* company.

Going Public (Private)

When a previously privately owned company offers its stock for sale to the public, it's *going public*. On rarer occasions, a company will buy its stock back — and *go private*.

IPO

Abbr.: **Initial Public Offer**. A company's first offer of stock for public sale.

Holding Company

Controls other companies through stock ownership, but doesn't engage directly in their productive operations.

Trading Company

A concept, esp. in the Orient, whereby a company controls R&D, raw materials, processing, manufacturing, marketing — and perhaps even the market (through trade agreements, etc.) — for their products.

● Corporation

Abbr.: **Corp. or Inc.** A legally created association of individuals with an existence independent of the members, and powers and liabilities distinct from theirs. The entity may enter into contracts, borrow, buy, sell, own property. *Corporate:* of a corporation. *Incorporate:* the *forming* of a corporation. *Incorporated:* chartered as a corporation and with its powers.

Incorporation is a popular structure due to liability being limited to the amount of the owners' investment; easy transfer of ownership through sale of stock; continuity of existence; ability to raise capital by sale of additional stock; shareholder's potential to profit if the business grows.

Conglomerate

A corporation made up of several subsidiary companies in unrelated industries; mergers and acquisitions may gain a corporation conglomerate status.

Merger

A legal combination of two or more companies by the transfer of properties to one surviving entity: the combining of two or more businesses into one.

Spin-off

A corporate reorganization whereby the capital stock of a division of a newly affiliated company is transferred to the parent corporation's stockholders, without any exchange of the parent's stock.

Subchapter S (Corporation)

A small business corporation with few shareholders. A simplified corporate charter that gives small businesses and individuals corporate tax benefits.

> *"Put all your eggs in one basket and—WATCH THAT BASKET."*
>
> *Andrew Carnegie*

● **Partnership**

> A business association of two or more partners in which resources are pooled and profits are shared. Also: the *state* of being a partner; the *relationship* between partners; the *contract* creating this relationship.

General Partner

> Has unlimited liability for a partnership's debts and obligations.

Joint Venture

> A business venture in which two or more companies enter a *temporary* partnership.

Limited Partnership

> Has one or more partners with limited liability because they don't participate in the partnership's affairs, but are only investors. There must be at least one general partner with full liability.

Silent Partner

> A financial partner taking no active part in the conduct of a business.

● **Proprietor (Proprietress)**

> Owner of a business establishment. The person who has the exclusive right of title.

Sole Proprietor

> A person who owns and manages a business alone; the business is called a *sole proprietorship*.

Buy and Hold

An investment strategy based on the idea that while there will be ups and downs in the market, the long term direction will be up. And holding a security for the long term will prove more profitable than trading in reaction to short term market movement.

Buy-Back

When a company buys back its own outstanding stock.

A buy-back is made when a company considers its own stock undervalued — a good investment; to take a publicly-held company private, for whatever reason; to take stock off the public market that might be bought by a hostile investor (read: takeover).

Buyers' Market

A market in which supply (of goods) is plentiful and the competition is tough, resulting in low prices. The opposite is a *sellers' market.*

Buying on Margin See: MARGIN

Buy Order

Instructions (for a fixed period of time, one week, etc.) to buy (a security, etc.).

Calender Year

A business that opens its books on January 1 and closes
them the following December 31, and is taxed accordingly,
is said to be on a calendar (business) year.   See also:
FISCAL YEAR

....

Call   See: OPTION

....

Capital

Money or property owned or used in business by an
individual, corporation, etc. Also *wealth used* to produce
more wealth.

Capital Gains (Losses)

Gains on invested capital; profit (or loss) on the sale of assets — stocks, bonds, real estate, etc.

Capital Gains Tax   See: TAX

Capital Goods

Assets (machinery, buildings, etc.) that are long term business investments, depreciated over a long time period.

> ***"Happiness is a positive cash flow."***
> *Fred Adler*

Capitalism

An economic system in which the means of production and distribution of products and wealth are privately owned and operated for profit. Esp.: contrasted to state-owned.

Capitalist

One who advocates capitalism. Also: one who has capital invested in business enterprises.

Capitalize

To furnish capital (for an enterprise). Also: 1) to *authorize* a certain amount of stock in a corporate charter; 2) to *issue stock as a dividend,* thereby capitalizing retained earnings.

Capitalization

Act of capitalizing. Also a corporation's *authorized* — or outstanding — stock.

Cartel

A group of individuals or businesses with a similar interest banded together to promote or improve that interest; may be by price-fixing, controlling supply or creating a monopoly. Ex.: OPEC.

....

▶ Cash

Money in the form of coins or banknotes (currency).
Of all assets, cash has highest liquidity with lowest risk.

....

Cash Account

A cash basis customer account with a brokerage firm.
See also: MARGIN ACCOUNT

....

Cash Cow

A business that generates excessive cash, over and above what's needed for its operating expenses.

....

Cash Flow

The pattern of a business' income and expenditures over a period of time (accounting period). The flow may be positive or negative.

....

Cash Method

Accounting: An accounting method based on the times actual (cash) payments are made and receipts are taken in. Also called *cash basis*. See also: ACCRUAL METHOD

....

Cashier's Check

A check drawn by a bank on its own funds, signed by its
cashier. Because it is a secure method of payment, a seller
may insist on a cashier's check if the amount is large or if
the buyer's identification or credit is unproven.

....

Casualty Insurance   See: INSURANCE
Central Bank   See: BANK

....

CEO

Abbr: **Chief Executive Officer.** The officer responsible
for a corporation's activities. An additional title usually
held by the chairman of the board or the president.

....

Certificate

Document provided with certain investments that sets
forth the terms of the investment and the rights and obligations of the buyer and seller. See also: BOND, CD, STOCK,
TREASURY

CD

Abbr: **Certificate of Deposit.** A form of savings
(offered by banks, S&Ls, etc.) with a fixed interest rate,
on a fixed amount, for a fixed time as stated on the certificate given the depositor. See also: TIME DEPOSIT

....

Chairman (of the Board of Directors)

A member of a corporation's board of directors who chairs
the board. The chairman is a corporation's highest ranking
officer, but may or may not have the highest executive
authority. Sometimes the title is honorary.

....

Chapters 7, 11   See: BANKRUPTCY
Chattel   See: MORTGAGE

....

Checking Account
    An account on deposit with a bank, S&L, etc., from which
    the depositor may withdraw funds by writing checks: a
    demand deposit account. See also: DEMAND DEPOSIT

....

Chemicals   See: DOW-JONES

> *"A broker is a man*
> *who runs your fortune*
> *into a shoestring."*
>   *Alexander Woollcott*

Churn(ing)
    High volume trading of a
    customer's stock, commodity,
    etc. account by the broker
    managing the account, in order
    to generate commissions—
    instead of representing the
    customer's best interests.
    If your broker makes more
    money on your account than
    you do, be suspicious.

....

Clearing House
    A place where mutual claims and accounts are settled
    (as between banks).

....

Closed Shop   See: UNION
Closely-Held Company   See: BUSINESS STRUCTURES
Closing   See: REAL ESTATE

> *"A fool and his money are soon parted."*
> *Old adage*

Closing Price
> The final price of a security at the end of a trading day.

Coin
> A piece of metal stamped and issued by a government for use as money — cash. Also: the *making* of coins.

Collateral
> Security pledged for the payment of a loan. Ex.: a house as collateral for the loan on it.

▶ **Collectible**
> An object judged worthy of collecting because of its value, uniqueness, scarcity; may also be attractive as an investment, or as a hedge against rising inflation. Also called a *collectors' item.* A group of collectibles is a *collection.* One who collects (collectibles) is a *collector.* (Also: a *bill collector.*) Collectibles have low liquidity, and are high risk. See also: COLLECTIBLES in earlier CATEGORIES OF MONEY section

● TYPES OF COLLECTIBLES

Antiques: Rare, old — usually more than 100 years old — furniture, silverware, etc.

Coins: Out of circulation coins in outstanding condition are favorite collectibles. Condition, date (and mint mark, for U.S. coins), metal content and size of the series issued determine value.

Gems: A cut and polished precious stone or pearl. A *gemstone* is a precious or semiprecious stone that can be cut and polished for use as a gem. A *colored gemstone* is any gemstone (colored or not) other than a diamond: emerald, opal, topaz, ruby, etc., etc. A *precious stone* is a gem distinguished for its beauty and rarity, hence, its value: diamond, emerald, ruby, etc. A *semiprecious stone* (amethyst, opal, topaz, etc.) is not as rare as a precious stone, but has commercial value for jewelry. *An investment grade diamond* is a stone so nearly flawless it's considered an investment, and will cost many times its jewelry value.

Oriental Rugs: Rugs characterized by knotted pile, hand made in Afghanistan, China, Iran, Morocco, Pakistan, Russia, Turkey. Oriental rugs as a group are sometimes mistakenly called Persian (Iranian) rugs.

Paintings, sculpture: One-of-a-kind art objects are very subjective collectibles — much of the value is in the eye of the beholder, which is as it should be.

....

Commerce
Trade, business. Large scale interchange of goods between regions or countries.

....

Commercial Real Estate   See: REAL ESTATE
Commercial Bank   See: BANK

....

Commission

Agents, sales representatives, etc., often provide their
services for a percentage of what they sell: they work
on commission.

....

▶ ## Commodity

An article of trade or commerce. In this context:
unprocessed or partially processed goods and certain
financial instruments *traded* on the world's commodity
exchanges. Commodity trading is considered speculative;
liquidity is medium, but risk is very high.

● ## TYPES OF TRADED COMMODITIES

Financials: Eurodollars, U.S. T-Bills, Treasury Bonds.
  Currencies: British pound, German mark, Japanese yen,
  Swiss franc.

Foods: Sugar, coffee, cocoa, orange juice.

Grains & Oils: Wheat, corn, soybeans, soybean oil,
soybean meal.

Industrials: Cotton, crude oil, lumber, heating oil,
unleaded gasoline.

Livestock & Meats: Cattle, feeder cattle, hogs, pork
bellies (bacon).

Metals: Copper, gold, platinum, silver.

Stock Indexes: Major Market Index, NYSE Composite
Index, Standard & Poors Composite Index, Value Line.

Commodity Exchange(s)

An exchange (place) where commodity future contracts
are bought and sold: **CBOT** — Chicago Board of Trade;
CME — Chicago Mercantile Exchange;

COMEX — Commodity Exchange New York;
KBOT — Kansas City Board of Trade; **NYCSCE** —
New York Coffee, Sugar & Cocoa Exchange;
NYCTN — New York Cotton Exchange; **NYME** —
New York Mercantile Exchange; **NYF** — New York
Futures Exchange.

*Not all commodities are
traded on all exchanges*

FUTURES KEY

Following each commodity is a key to the exchange on which it is traded. The minimum contract size and the monetary units represented appear on the next line. The exchanges are: **CBOT**—Chicago Board of Trade, **CME**—Chicago Mercantile Exchange, **COMEX**—Commodity Exchange New York, **KBOT**—Kansas City Board of Trade, **NYCSCE**—New York Coffee, Sugar & Cocoa Exchange, **NYCTN**—New York Cotton Exchange, **NYME**—New York Mercantile Exchange, **NYF**—New York Futures Exchange.

Commodity Futures Contract

An agreement to take or make delivery of a specified
amount of a traded commodity, at a specified price,
on a specified *future* date.

The Contract is secured by the deposit of a percentage
(10 to 20%, usually) of the contract's total value. This
percentage is called the margin. The transaction
is called *trading on margin.* See also: MARGIN

Commodity Futures Trading

Buying a contract is called *going long* (or *buying long*);
selling one is *going short.* Also called selling short —
you sell something you don't have: you have a *short
contract.* When you own a long or short contract, you
have a *position* in the market. You're trading.

A trader who doesn't want to take or make delivery
of a contract cancels it by taking (buying) an opposite
position, *covering* a long contract with a short, or vice-
versa. Less than 5% of commodities traded exist—
the rest are just paper: trades.

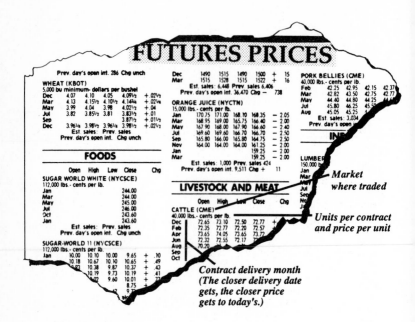

FUTURES PRICES

Prev. day's open int. 286 Chg unch

WHEAT (KBOT)
5,000 bu minimum- dollars per bushel

	Open	High	Low	Close	Chg
Dec	4.07	4.10	4.05	4.09½	+.02½
Mar	4.13	4.15½	4.10½	4.14¼	+.02¼
May	3.99	4.04	3.98	4.02½	+.04
Jul	3.82	3.85½	3.81	3.83½	+.01
Sep				3.87½	+.01½
Dec	3.96¼	3.98½	3.96¼	3.98½	+.02½

Est. sales: Prev. sales
Prev. day's open int. Chg unch

FOODS

	Open	High	Low	Close	Chg
SUGAR WORLD WHITE (NYCSCE)					
112,000 lbs.- cents per lb.					
Jan				244.00	
Mar				244.00	
May				245.00	
Jul				246.00	
Oct				243.60	
Jan				243.60	

Est. sales: Prev. sales
Prev. day's open int. Chg unch

SUGAR-WORLD 11 (NYCSCE)
112,000 lbs.- cents per lb.

	Open	High	Low	Close	Chg
Jan	10.00	10.10	10.00	9.65	+.10
	10.18	10.67	10.10	10.65	+.49
	10.23	10.38	9.87	10.37	+.43
	10.19	9.73	10.19	+.41	
	9.60	10.01	+		
			8.75		
			9		

Dec	1490	1515	1490	1500	+	15
Mar	1515	1528	1515	1522	+	16

Est. sales: 6,448 Prev. sales 6,406
Prev. day's open int. 36,470 Chg — 738

ORANGE JUICE (NYCTN)
15,000 lbs.- cents per lb.

	Open	High	Low	Close	Chg
Jan	170.75	171.00	168.10	168.35	— 2.05
Mar	168.95	169.00	165.75	166.40	— 2.00
May	167.90	168.00	167.90	166.60	— 2.40
Jul	169.60	169.60	166.70	166.70	— 2.50
Sep	165.80	166.00	165.80	164.75	— 2.50
Nov	164.00	164.00	164.00	161.25	— 2.00
Jan				159.25	— 2.00
Mar				159.25	— 2.00

Est. sales: 1,000 Prev. sales 424
Prev. day's open int. 9,511 Chg + 11

LIVESTOCK AND MEAT

	Open	High	Low	Close	Chg
CATTLE (CME)					
40,000 lbs.- cents per lb.					
Dec	72.65	73.10	72.50	72.77	—
Feb	73.35	72.77	72.20	72.57	—
Apr	73.65	74.05	73.65	73.77	—
Jun	72.32	72.55	72.17	72	—
Aug	70.20				
Sep					
Oct					

PORK BELLIES (CME)
40,000 lbs.- cents per lb.

	Open	High	Low	Close	Chg
Feb	42.25	42.95	42.15	42.37	
Mar	42.82	43.50	42.75	42.77	
May	44.40	44.80	44.25		
Jul	45.80	46.25	45.5		
Aug	45.05	45.25	4		

Est. sales: 3,034
Prev. day's open i

IN

LUMBER
150,000 b
Jan
Mar
Jul
Sep
No

Market where traded

Units per contract and price per unit

Contract delivery month (The closer delivery date gets, the closer price gets to today's.)

Commodity Trader

One who trades commodities. A *day trader* is a commodity trader who completes all trades in the same day, finishing with an account balance at zero. Also called an *in-and-out trader*.

....

Common Stock See: STOCK

Common Market See: EEC (EUROPEAN ECONOMIC
COMMUNITY)

....

Community Property

Property acquired by a husband and wife, singly or together, that is considered by law in some states (community property states) to be jointly owned, and shared, should divorce separate the couple.

....

Company See: BUSINESS STRUCTURES

Compound Interest See: INTEREST

Comprehensive Insurance See: INSURANCE

Computerized Trading See: PROGRAMMED TRADING

Condominium See: REAL ESTATE

Conglomerate See: BUSINESS STRUCTURES

Consumer Goods

Goods that are used up (consumed) to satisfy people's needs — food, clothing, etc.

> *"Money—in its absence we are coarse; in its presence we are vulgar."*
> *Mignon McLaughlin*

Consortium

Association, partnership, union: a combination of interested groups for the purpose of setting up a financial operation that requires large capital resources.

Contract

An agreement — esp. written and enforceable by law — between two or more parties. Also the *written document*.

Contrarian Theory

An investment strategy of doing the opposite of what the rest of a market (stock, real estate, etc.) is doing: buying when everyone else is selling, and vice-versa. J. Paul Getty supposedly was an advocate of contrarian theory.

....

Convertible   See: BOND, INSURANCE, STOCK
Corporation   See: BUSINESS STRUCTURE

....

Correction

Up/down change in a company's stock price to more realistically represent the company's actual value.

....

Coupon Bond   See: BOND

"So far as my coin would stretch; and where it would not, I have used my credit."
Shakespeare

▶ Credit

The confidence of a seller in a
buyer's ability (and intention) to pay,
as demonstrated by entrusting that buyer with
goods, without receiving immediate payment.
One who extends the credit is a *creditor*.

Credit Bureau (Credit Agency)

A firm that investigates the credit status of its clients' customers and assigns them credit ratings.

Credit Card

A (plastic) card that entitles the owner named to bill merchandise to a charge account. Also sometimes called *plastic*. Interest is charged for the service.

Credit Line (Line of Credit)

The maximum amount of credit a store, bank, etc. authorizes a customer.

Credit Rating

A classification of credit risk, based on investigation (by a credit bureau), of a customer's financial resources, prior history and pattern of debt payments.

Credit Risk

The likelihood of a borrower defaulting on a loan. Also a would-be *borrower who is likely to default*.

Credit Union

A cooperative group (usually employees of the credit union's sponsoring body — a company, union, etc.) that holds members' savings accounts, CDs, etc. and pays interest on those deposits. Credit unions also make loans to members at attractive interest rates, and may offer credit cards, mortgages, etc. Credit unions are owned by members who vote on their policies.

Share Account

A savings account in a credit union; a *share certificate* is a certificate of deposit issued by a credit union.

Currency

Paper money issued by the government of a country.

Currency Exchange

A place — an official government franchise, a bank or another private enterprise — where the currency of one country can be exchanged for that of another. For the service, the exchange charges a fee.

Currency Fluctuation

Refers to the changing value of a national currency in relation to the currencies of other nations.

....

Customer's Man/Woman   See: ACCOUNT EXECUTIVE

....

Cycle

In this context the economy's expansion-recession cycle. Several years of expansion, a *peak*, followed by a year or more of contraction, typifies past cycles — then it begins again. There is also a *megacycle* of about fifty years' duration, which supposedly concludes in severe economic depression. Also called the *business cycle*.

Accounting Cycle

One year — January 1 through December 31.

Cyclical (Sales, Stock)

While most businesses and securities react to the economic cycle, some react to other cycles as well. Ex.: agricultural companies may be sensitive to crop seasons. Farmers buy new tractors before the spring planting season begins, or after the fall harvest (for tax savings), so a tractor company's sales — and its stock — may be hottest at those times, year in and year out: it's *cyclical*. Such companies often diversify into other product areas to try to level out the cycle.

WHO GOES WITH HOW MUCH?

Jackson: $20.

Franklin: $100.

Grant: $50.

Washington: $1.

Lincoln: $5.

Hamilton: $10.

There were also $500, $1000, $5000, $10,000 and even $100,000 bills! But in 1969 they were taken out of circulation. The risk of carrying large cash sums, expanded use of credit, and fast electronic credit checks contributed to the demise of the big bills.

D&B

Abbr.: **Dun and Bradstreet Corp.** A credit rating/
reporting service. To *run a D&B* refers to getting
a (customer's) credit rating from Dun and Bradstreet.

Day Trader   See: COMMODITIES

DBA

Abbr.: **Doing Business As.** A company or individual
using a name other than its own for business purposes.

Debenture

Debt backed only by the borrower's integrity; ex.: an
unsecured bond.

Debt

Something owed or that one is bound to pay to another. Also: *being obligated* — in debt. *Debtor:* one who is in debt — opposite of *creditor*. See also: CREDIT

Debt Retirement

Paying off a debt. *Debt service:* the yearly amount required to pay interest and principal due on a debt.

Debt to Equity Ratio

The debt owed by a company divided into its equity (value).

Decreasing Term   See: INSURANCE
Deductible   See: INSURANCE, TAX

Deed

A document executed under seal and delivered to effect a transfer; esp. real estate. Also the *act of transferring* by deed.

Default

Failure to satisfy a debt or obligation. Ex.: he didn't pay his car loan and therefore defaulted on it. Also: *failure to make a court appearance* as instructed.

"*There are poor men in this country who cannot be bought; the day I found that out, I sent my gold abroad.*"
Jules Bertillon

Deferred (Payment, Tax)

Postponed, delayed; suspended or withheld for or until a certain time, or even permanently.

Deficit

The amount by which a sum of money falls short of the amount required, as in the operation of a business or a government.

Deficit Spending

The practice of spending more money than comes in, esp. by governments.

Deflation

A fall in the general price levels or a contraction of credit and available money: opposite of *inflation*.

Defraud

To take something by fraud; ex.: he defrauded his firm of millions. See also: FRAUD

Demand

Economics: The desire to buy, combined with the money to do so. Also: the *amount* of goods buyers will take at a particular price.   See also: SUPPLY

Demand Deposit

A deposit subject to withdrawal at the demand of the depositor without prior notice is payable *on demand*. Ex.: a checking account.

On Demand

Due when the lender asks for payment, such as a demand loan or note.

Dependent

A child, spouse, parent, etc. one supports financially
(totally or in large part). See also: TAX

....

Depreciation

Business: A slow expensing of assets (of hard assets,
machinery, etc.) because of use and wear, decline in price
etc. Also: deduction allowed when computing the property's
value for taxes. *Depreciate:* The act — to claim a
property's depreciation (for tax benefits).   See also:
AMORTIZE, TAX

Accelerated Depreciation

Allows greater depreciation in the early years of an
item's expected (use) life, and decreasing amounts in
later years. The result is an earlier tax write-off than
when the straight-line method is used.

Straight-Line Depreciation

Calculated by simply dividing item cost by expected
years of use. For taxes, the same amount is depreciated
each year.

Depreciation, Currency: A decrease — depreciation —
in the purchasing or exchange value of a nation's money.

....

Depression

Economics: A period during which business activity,
employment and security markets' values severely decline
or remain at a very low level.

Great Depression

The worldwide economic crisis and period of low business activity, beginning with the U.S. stock market
crash in October 1929 and continuing through much of
the 1930s.

....

> *"All work and no play makes jack."*
> **Anonymous**

Deregulate

Removal of government regulatory controls from an industry, a commodity, etc. Ex.: to deregulate the airline or trucking industries; they undergo *deregulation.*

Devaluate

To reduce the value of, devalue.

Devaluation

A government's official reduction of its currency's exchange value, relative to other country's currencies, in the attempt to encourage exports, tourism, etc.

Direct Tax   See: TAX

Diamond   See: COLLECTIBLE

Director

One (of a group) chosen to direct the affairs of a corporation.   See also: BOARD OF DIRECTORS

Disability   See: INSURANCE

Discount

Finance: To buy or sell a note before it matures, at a reduced price based on the interest remaining to be earned (until its maturity). Also: 1) deducting interest on a loan at the time the loan is made; 2) the act.

Discount, Trade: An amount deducted from an item's usual price.

Discount Bond   See: BOND

Discount Broker   See: BROKER

Discount Rate

Rate of interest federal reserve banks charge on money loaned to member banks. (Government securities are usually collateral for these loans.)

....

Discretionary Income

The part of a person's income remaining *after deductions* for taxes, etc. Also called *disposable income.*

....

Disinflation

Slow down of the rate at which prices increase — usually during a recession; because sales are dropping, retailers can't pass on higher costs to consumers. See also: DEFLATION, INFLATION

....

Diversification

The manufacturing of a variety of products, selling various merchandise, investing in several securities, etc., so that a failure or slump in one area won't be disastrous to the total venture. *Vertical diversification* refers to branching out in the same general area of business, while *horizontal diversification* means going into entirely new business areas.

Diversified Portfolio

Securities of various types and risk levels, assembled to maximize opportunity while minimizing the effect of adverse economic changes.

....

Divest

To sell off. *Divesture:* the act.

....

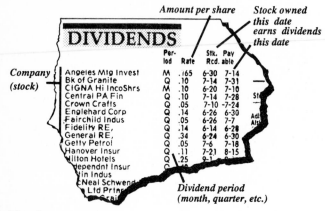

Dividends

Finance: The per-share earnings a corporation pays to its shareholders.

Dividends, Insurance: Participating insurance. A distribution is made to policyholders of a part of the premiums not required to cover the company's claims and expenses.

....

Double Indemnity   See: INSURANCE

....

Dow-Jones (& Company)

A financial and business reporting/publishing firm.

Dow-Jones Average

Refers to the Dow-Jones 30 Stock Industrial Average: *The Dow* — the most watched and quoted index. Dow-Jones also daily compiles a 20 stock Transportation Average and a 15 stock Utility Average. Together they are called the (Dow) *65 Stock Average*.

Drawing Account

An account used by a partner, employee, etc. for cash withdrawals; an account charged with advances of money for expenses or salaries, against earnings, esp. for sales representatives. Also called a *Draw*.

Dumping

Selling goods in large quantities, at low prices, without regard to the effect on market conditions. Also selling goods in foreign markets *below* costs, to promote exports or to damage foreign competition.

Durable Goods

Goods such as household appliances, machinery, sports equipment, etc., that aren't consumable or disposable and can be used for several years. Also called *hard goods* or *durables*.

Duty

A tax on imports and exports. *Duty-Free* means without duty.

Earnest Money

Money given by buyer to a seller to bind a contract;
a deposit.

Early Retirement (Benefits)

Retirement from a position at an age earlier than normal,
with benefits proportionately reduced. To decrease its
workforce, a company may encourage senior employees
to take retirement by offering them attractive early retirement benefits.

Early Withdrawal Penalty

Funds deposited for an agreed period (as in a CD, time
deposit, etc.), but withdrawn before the period has elapsed,
which may incur a penalty; usually a deduction from interest
already earned.

Earnings

Money earned; wages; profits — individual or corporate.

Chart is self-explanatory. Most financial reports are in the currency of the country where the company is chartered, so an exchange rate may have to be used to get dollar figures from foreign results.

Price-Earnings Ratio

Abbr.: **P/E Ratio**: Per share earnings of a security, divided into the current price of that security.

EPS

Abbr.: **Earnings Per Share**. The net income of a corporation divided by the number of shares of its common stock outstanding.

Earnings Statement

A formal corporate statement of EPS (or lack of), usually with an explanation of the result.

Economics

The science (art?) dealing with models of production, distribution and consumption of goods and services. Also: financial considerations; *economically significant aspects*. An *economist* practices economics.

Economy

A system of production and distribution of wealth. Esp. a country's resource management, as regards national productivity.

EEC

Abbr.: **European Economic Community.**   Also called
the *Common Market.*   The Western European economic
association created to end trade barriers among member
nations; to adopt common import duties on goodsfrom
countries outside the Community; to ease movement
and workers' rights for member countries' citizens.

Belgium, Denmark, France, Greece, Ireland, Italy,
Luxembourg, Netherlands, Portugal, Spain, U.K., and
West Germany are EEC members, at this writing.

EMS

Abbr.: **European Monetary System.** A Common
Market program to reduce fluctuation of Western European currencies against one another.

> *"Wealth—any income that is at least
> one hundred dollars more a year
> than the income of one's wife's
> sister's husband."*   H.L. Mencken

Embargo

A government-imposed
restriction on trade (of
all products or specified
products) with other
nations. Also: such a
restriction on interstate
freight transportation.

Endow

> To provide with a permanent fund or source of income.
> Ex.: to endow a college. An *endowment* is a gift, grant,
> bequest — the property, funds, etc. endowed.
>
> **Endowment Insurance**   See: INSURANCE

Entrepreneur

> A person who organizes and manages any enterprise,
> esp., a business, usually with considerable initiative and
> risk. A businessperson who hopes to earn a high gain for
> the risk taken.

Equity

> The value of a property or business beyond mortgages,
> claims, liens, etc. owed on it. Also: *stock* (not bonds)
> held by a corporation's shareholders. See also: STOCK

Escrow

> The deposit of something, e.g., money, property, to be held
> as security with a (state regulated) third party until the
> terms of a contract are met. Ex.: money placed *in escrow:*
> with a third person. Also: *an agreement* providing for
> the deposit.

Estate

> Property or possessions; the property of a person deceased.
>
> **Estate Planning**
>> Organizing one's affairs and property to maximize value,
>> while minimizing the tax heirs must pay.
>
> **Estate Tax**   See: TAX

Estimated Tax   See: TAX

....

Eurodollars.

U.S. dollars held outside the U.S., especially in European banks.

....

Exchange Rate

Ratio at which a unit of one country's currency can be exchanged for the currency of another country.

Ex.: 2DM = $1, $1 = 5FF, etc. Depending on the rate, a currency is said to be *strong* or *weak*.

FOREIGN MONEY

	Fgn.currency in dollars		Dollar in Fgn.currency		
	Thu.	Wed.	Thu.	Wed.	Isra
f-Argent	.0053	.0055	190.56	180.64	Italy
Australia	.7395	.7447	1.3520	1.3482	Japan
Austria	.0696	.0703	14.36	14.23	30-dy
c-Belgium	.0234	.0236	42.70	42.31	60-dy
Brazil	.7457	.8039	1.3410	1.2439	90
Britain	1.5420	1.5153	.6485	.6599	
30-day fwd	1.5362	1.5092	.6510	.6826	
60-day fwd	1.5295	1.5029	.6538	.6654	
90-day fwd	1.5240	1.4958	.6566		
Canada	.8358	.8342	1.19		
30-day fwd	.8336	.8319			

Exchange rate of the day, and the day before. 30, 60, 90-day fwd (forward) refers to rates on the currency futures market..

....

Exchange   See: COMMODITIES, MARKET, STOCK
Excise Tax   See: TAX
Exempt   See: TAX

....

Expense

A (business) cost or charge.

Expense Account

An employee's account (or record) of business-related expenses, e.g., travel, hotel, meals, entertainment to be reimbursed by the employer.

....

Export

To send goods, commodities, ideas, etc., to other countries for sale, exchange. Also: the item *exported*.

"Ready money is Aladdin's lamp."
Byron

Face Value

Value printed on the face of a stock, bill, document, etc.

....

Factory

One or more buildings with facilities for manufacturing goods.

Factory Orders

Orders received by manufacturers during a specified time period; a measure of the strength of the economy.

Factory Price

Price quoted for manufactured goods picked up at the factory gate, before handling and shipping costs.

....

Family of Funds   See: MUTUAL FUND

....

Fannie Mae
> Any of the publicly traded securities collateralized by a pool of mortgages backed by the *Federal National Mortgage Association. Abbr.:* **FNMA** — Fannie Mae.

....

Farm   See: REAL ESTATE

....

FDIC
> *Abbr.:* **Federal Deposit Insurance Corporation.** A public corporation that insures FDIC member banks' customers' deposits (accounts) for up to $100,000.

....

FHA
> *Abbr.:* **Federal Housing Administration.** A government agency that helps homeowners finance the purchase and repair of their homes. An original goal of the FHA was to stimulate housing construction.

....

Federal Reserve System
> U.S. federal banking system: a central bank (*Federal Reserve Bank*) in each of 12 districts, controlled by a central board of governors (*Federal Reserve Board*).

> **(The) FED**
>> Acronym for the Federal Reserve System and the Board. The FED has wide powers in controlling credit and the flow of money, and in regulating and supervising member banks.

> **FED Watchers**
>> Those who observe the Federal Reserve Board's policies and actions, anticipating the affects on the security and commodity markets.

> **Federal Reserve Note**
>> Paper money issued by a Federal Reserve Bank.

....

Fee

A charge for professional services; e.g., doctor's fee, accountant's fee, etc.

....

Fee Simple

Absolute ownership of land with no restrictions as to selling it or giving it away.

....

Fiat

An authoritative decree, sanction or order. Also an *arbitrary decree* by a person or group having absolute authority to enforce it.

Fiat Money

Paper currency made legal tender by a fiat of the government, but not based on precious metal, nor convertible to it. With the end of the gold standard and silver in coins, U.S. currency became fiat money, as are the currencies of most other countries.

....

Fiduciary

A person to whom property or power is entrusted for the benefit of another; in the nature of trust and confidence, as in public affairs.

"I've been rich
and I've been poor;
rich is better."

Sophie Tucker

Finance

The management of revenues; the conduct or transaction of money matters generally, esp. banking and investment.
Finances: monetary resources, money, capital.
Financial: pertaining to money, credit, etc.

Financial Consultant

One who is presumably knowledgable in such matters, who consults with clients and makes recommendations on managing their financial affairs.

Financial Instrument

Stocks, bonds, T-bills, CDs, etc. — any document that is negotiable and represents a legal claim on money.

Financial Planning

Devising a program to best manage finances and capital through budgeting, investment, etc. Also, the business: developing such programs by a *financial planner*.

Financier

One engaged (and hopefully skilled) in managing large public or corporate financial operations.

....

Finance Company

A company that makes loans to consumers; buys accounts receivable; discounts installment contracts; gives credit to retailers and manufacturers.

Finance Charge

Interest paid for borrowing money or buying on credit.

....

Financial Wire   See: WIRESERVICE
Financial Analyst   See: INVESTMENT ANALYST

....

Fine Print

Detailed legal wording of a contract, lease, policy, etc., set in type smaller than the body of the document. May contain restrictions or qualifications.

....

Fire & Theft   See: INSURANCE

First Mortgage   See: MORTGAGE

....

Fiscal

Pertaining to financial matters in general.

Fiscal Policy

Policies pertaining to the public treasury and revenues.

Fiscal Year

Any period of one year during which an organization's financial results are measured, not necessarily a calendar year.

....

Fixed Income

A uniform rate of income. Ex.: a security that pays a set rate of interest over a long period. Retired people living on pensions are on fixed incomes which remain relatively the same, month in and month out.

....

Fixed Annuity   See: INSURANCE

Fixed Asset   See: ASSET

Fixed Rate   See: MORTGAGE

....

Flat Economy

The economy is horizontal — not moving up or down, boring, nothing dramatic or interesting is happening.

....

> ## *"The only question about wealth is what you do with it."*
> *John D. Rockefeller, Jr.*

Float

To be launched.

Float, Banking: Uncollected checks and commercial paper in transfer (launched and floating) from bank to bank. Most of us have used the float: the time it takes after we write a check for it to get back to our bank. *Caution*: electronics and new laws make transfers faster and float time shorter than it used to be.

Float, Corporate: Launching a company, a bond or stock issue, etc. Ex.: a company floats a bond issue, makes its bonds available for public sale.

Float, Currency: Allowed to fluctuate freely, i.e., to float in the foreign-exchange market, valued according to demand, instead of being exchanged at a fixed rate.

....

Forbes 400, 500

Forbes magazine's annual lists of the 400 wealthiest individuals in the U.S. and the country's 500 largest publicly held companies. See also MONEY MEDIA section

....

Foreclose See: MORTGAGE
....

Foreign Debt

Money owed to another country, resulting from a loan or from a deficit balance of trade.

....

FDI

Abbr.: **Foreign Direct Investment.** Capital invested
by private individuals or groups from one country in the
businesses, property, land, etc. of another country.

....

Foreign Exchange

Financial instruments — checks, currency, bills of exchange, etc. — used for transactions between the businesses
of different countries.

....

> *"Though mothers and
> fathers give us life,
> it is money alone
> which preserves it."*
> **Japanese Proverb**

....

Fortune 500

Fortune magazine's annual list of the 500 largest U.S.
industrial companies. See also MONEY MEDIA Section.

....

Franchise

The license granted to an individual or group by a company
to market its products or services in a specific territory.
Also: a *store, etc.*, operating under such a license, and the
territory covered by the license.

Franchise Fee (tax) See: TAX

....

Fraud

Deceit, trickery or breach of confidence, in order to gain profit or unfair advantage.

Freddie Mac

A publicly traded security that represents participation in a pool of mortgages guaranteed by the *Federal Home Loan Mortgage Corporation. Abbr.:* **FHLMC** — Freddie Mac.

Free Trade

Trade between countries, free from governmental duties or restrictions. Also: 1) *international trade* free from protective duties, subject only to revenue tariffs; 2) the *system* of such trade.

Free Lunch

Something given with no expectation of repayment; rumor has it there is no such thing.

Freelance

To sell work or services by the hour, day or job rather than working for a salary. The term comes from the time when mercenaries, free of obligation to any specific feudal lord, hired out their lance to the highest bidder: *freelancers.*

Freeze

To fix rents, prices, etc. at a specific level, usually by government order. To stop or limit production, etc.

Friendly Takeover   See: TAKEOVER

Front-Load   See: MUTUAL FUND

FSLIC

Abbr.: **Federal Savings & Loan Insurance Corporation.**
Federal agency that insures depositors' funds in member
savings and loans.

....

Full Service   See: BANK

Fundamental Analysis   See: INVESTMENT ANALYSIS

....

Funny Money

Securities: Of questionable value, used in corporate LBOs.

Currency: Of little value — such as a nation's currency that
has been artificially inflated or devaluated. Also: *counterfeit*
currency.   See also: PIK

....

Futures   See: COMMODITIES

Gem   See: COLLECTIBLES

....

General Ledger

    A business' main book of accounts, where all financial
transactions are recorded and proved by trial balances.

....

General Obligation Bond   See: BOND
General Partner   See: BUSINESS STRUCTURE
Gift Tax   See: TAX

....

Ginny Mae

    A bond or certificate sold by the *Government National
Mortgage Association. Abbr.:* **GNMA** — Ginny Mae.

....

Glamor Stock   See: STOCK

....

Global Stock Market

The world's major markets — New York, London, Tokyo, etc. — considered together as one big market.

Glut

Oversupply: too much. Ex.: the oil glut, when producers flooded world markets with so much petroleum that oil prices plummeted.

GNP

Abbr.: **Gross National Product**. The total value of goods and services a nation produces during a certain time period (usually one year). Ex.: this year's U.S. *GNP*.

> *"Nothing is more admirable than the fortitude with which millionaires tolerate the disadvantages of their wealth."*
> — *Rex Stout*

Gnomes of Zurich

The Swiss banking community, in general, the community's very affluent Zurich branch, in particular.

Going Public (Private)

See: BUSINESS STRUCTURE

Gold See: METALS

Gold Certificate

An obsolete U.S. currency that was redeemable in gold
for the stated face value. See also SILVER CERTIFICATE

Gold Standard

A monetary system backed by gold, in which currency can
be converted to gold; it provided a common exchange basis
for various currencies. (Ended in the U.S. in 1971.)

Gold Basis: A gold standard as a basis for prices.

Golden Parachute

An employment agreement that guarantees a company
executive severance pay and benefits, should his/her job be
terminated as a result of the company's sale or merger.

Golden Handshake

An incentive — generous severance pay, pension benefits, etc.— offered an older employee as an incentive to
retire early.

Goods   See: CAPITAL GOODS, CONSUMER GOODS, DURABLE
GOODS, SEMI-DURABLE GOODS

Government Bonds   See: TREASURY

Grace Period

The period after a loan or insurance payment falls due —
but is not paid — until a penalty, late charge or cancellation
goes into effect.

GI (Gross Income)   See: INCOME

Gross Profit   See: PROFIT

Group Insurance   See: INSURANCE

Growth Industry (Stock, Company, etc.)

An industry, security or business expected to grow in value
faster than average, over a long period of time.

Growth Fund   See: MUTUAL FUND

Growth & Income Fund   See: MUTUAL FUND

> *"Nothing is a greater proof*
> *of a narrow and grovelling disposition*
> *than to be fond of money,*
> *while nothing is more noble and exalted*
> *than to despise it, if thou hast it not;*
> *and if thou hast it, to employ it*
> *in beneficence and liberality."*
>
> *Cicero*

Hard Money

Money made of metal, not paper: coins.

....

Head & Shoulders

A pattern that occurs on security analysts' charts.

....

Headhunter

A personnel recruiter for a corporation or executive placement agency. Also: a *recruitment agency*.

....

Health Insurance   See: INSURANCE

....

Heavy Industry

Basic industry — steel, manufacturing, mining, etc., (as compared to *light industry* — electronics, computers, etc.). Also called *smokestack industry*.

Hedging

Entering into transactions to protect against loss in other transactions, through a compensatory price movement.

High-Rise   See: REAL ESTATE
High-Grade Bond   See: BOND

High-Tech

High technology, requiring sophisticated methods, techniques, equipment such as computers. Also: the *products, companies, stock*.

Highs & Lows

The high and low prices of securities during a trading period.

HMO

Abbr.: **Health Maintenance Organization**. A comprehensive health services plan, prepaid by an individual or employer, which provides members with preventive care, treatment and hospitalization in a central health center.

Holding Company   See: BUSINESS STRUCTURES
Homeowners' Insurance   See: INSURANCE
Hostile Takeover   See: TAKEOVER
House Call   See: MARGIN

Housing Starts

The number of residential building starts during a period, usually a month. An indication of the national economy's general strength.

....

Hub

An exchange trading floor surrounded by cubicles wired to brokerage houses to execute trades.

> *"Money is like muck, not good unless spread."*
>
> *Francis Bacon*

IMF

   Abbr.: **International Monetary Fund.** Created in 1944,
   the IMF promotes international monetary cooperation, and,
   by lending foreign currencies in exchange for a nation's
   own currency, helps stabilize the balance of payments.

....

Import

   To bring something — goods, services, customs, etc. — into
   one country from another.

....

Income

   All money and other items of value taken in during a certain
   time period by a person or business for work, services,
   business sales, from investments, etc.

GI

Abbr.: **Gross Income.**   The total business revenue received before deductions for rent, cost of goods sold, taxes, etc. Also called *gross revenue.*

(Net) Income

What's left after deducting expenses and taxes from GI.

....

Income Fund   See: MUTUAL FUND
Income Property   See: REAL ESTATE

....

Income Statement

An income and expense accounting that indicates a company's net profit/loss over a period, usually a year.

....

Income Tax   See: TAX
Index   See: STOCK

....

Indicators

Those things, positive or negative, which indicate the strength and direction of the economy. Ex.: inflation, interest and employment rates, strength of currency, balance of trade, industrial production, consumer sales, etc.

Leading Indicator

Economic indexes (unemployment rate, new business investment, stock prices, etc.) that change *before* the general economy changes, and indicate a coming shift in business activity.

Lagging Indicator

Unit labor costs, prime interest rate, etc. which show no major change until *after* the economy has changed, and signify the end of a period in the *business cycle.*

....

Indirect Tax   See: TAX
Industrials   See: DOW-JONES

....

Inflation

When the amount of money in circulation dramatically
increases, accompanied by sharply rising product and
service prices. Also called an *over-heated economy:*
there's too much activity. See also: DEFLATION,
DISINFLATION, STAGFLATION

Inflationary (Pressures)

The underlying reasons for increased money in circulation
and rising prices (inflation): savings withdrawn and spent;
buying on credit; currency sales by foreign governments;
additional currency printed by the government to pay bills
so that a sudden sharp drop in the currency's value results.

Inflation Rate

The percentage inflation increases over a period of time.
Inflationary spiral: continuing, accelerating price rises for
goods and services, attributed to increasing wage and
production costs.

*"One of the benefits
of inflation is that a
kid can no longer get
sick on a nickel's
worth of candy."*
Journeyman Barber magazine

Inheritance

Money or property inherited or to be inherited; received
by laws of inheritance from an ancestor at their death.
Ownership by birthright.

Inheritance Tax   See: TAX

....

Insider Trading

Trading of securities by a corporate executive, an involved
broker, their relatives, friends, etc., who *by nature of
position* have inside information about the corporation and
its plans. And who *take advantage* of what they know in
order to profit, before the information becomes public.
Unethical, illegal. Ex.: an executive who knows of a
pending merger between his/her company and another,
and uses the knowledge to trade the corporations' stock.

....

Insolvent

When you can't pay the bills and debts you owe, you're
insolvent, in a state of *insolvency* — broke, busted!

....

Installment (Buying, Selling)

A deferred sale/payment plan which lets a buyer make
a partial payment at the time of purchase, and pay the
remaining balance in equal periodic (usually monthly)
payments: installments. Interest on the unpaid balance
is charged, and a contract states the transaction's terms.

....

Institutional Investors

Very large investors: banks, insurance companies, corporate
or union pension funds, etc.

Institutional Buying/Selling

Institutional securities trading: the term heard on the evening news as a partial explanation for big up or down swings in the stock market prices. See also: BLOCK BUYING/SELLING, PROGRAMMED TRADING

▶ ## Insurance

An agreement made by contract and for a fee in which one party (*insurer*) agrees to cover a second (*insured*) party's loss of life or property or legal liability, should such loss occur, and to reimburse the insured for the loss in the amount agreed upon. When you buy insurance, you pay someone to share your risks.

Insurance Agent

One who represents an insurance company, sells the company's products and provides its customers assistance and service. An agent represents one company, while an *insurance broker* sells several companies' products.

Insurance Policy

The document that establishes the terms contracted between the insurer and the insured.

Beneficiary

The person named to receive the benefits from an insured's life insurance policy.

Deductible

An amount specified in a policy which an insured must pay before the insurance company becomes liable for payment on losses or injuries. Ex.: on a health plan with a $500 deductible, the insured pays the first $500, and the insurance company pays claims above $500. (Doesn't apply to life insurance.)

Option

The right of the beneficiary (or the insured) to determine
the intervals and the amount in which benefits shall be
paid. (Life insurance only.)

Policyholder

The insured; one in whose name a policy is written.

Policy Loan

Loan to a policyholder with the built-up cash value as
security. *Cash value:* the amount of cash accumulated in
equity-building life policies, which may be borrowed
against or withdrawn. *Loan value:* the amount of money
that can be borrowed against a policy, based on its cash
value. (Life insurance only.)

> *"Wealthy people miss one of life's greatest*
> *thrills—paying the last installment."*
>
> *Anonymous*

Policy Premium

Periodic payments an insured
makes to an insurer for risk
coverage. Premium rates are
based on *actuarial (experience)
tables* and risk calculations
(made by actuaries) which
consider value, conditions,
hazards, life style, age (life
expectancy), etc. and other
risk-determining factors.

Waiver of Premium

A policy provision which specifies conditions under
which life insurance premium payments may be skipped
(waived) due to illness, disability, etc.

Short-Rate

When a policy is cancelled with paid-up time remaining on it, part of the premium may be rebated, minus a penalty for not fulfilling the contract. The policyholder is *short-rated*.

Policy Rider

An amendment to a policy — usually limiting liability under specific conditions. Ex.: if one has a heart condition, a life insurance policy rider may exclude liability for death resulting from this condition.

Policy Surrender

The giving up of a life insurance policy by the owner, for its accumulated value: *surrender value*. See also CASH VALUE

Insure

To afford security; to cover a risk with insurance. Also: to issue or buy insurance.

Insurer

A company that insures. Also called 1) an insurance carrier; 2) an underwriter.

"The rich were dull and they drank too much."
Ernest Hemingway

● **TYPES OF INSURANCE**

Accident: Insurance against property loss or damage, or personal injury due to accident.

Automobile: Liability, property damage, medical, collision, and comprehensive insurance.

> *No-Fault:* Automobile insurance designed to let the policyholder promptly collect for a loss from his own insurance company, without determination of liability. Not available in all states.

Business: Insurance on a business — liability, contents, etc. Also, there are coverages such as malpractice policies for doctors that cover the risks unique to certain professions or businesses.

Casualty: Coverage against lawsuits from accidents, property damage, etc.

Disability: Insures income, should the insured become disabled and lose earning power. Available from private companies or state governments; Social Security also has disability benefits.

Group: Life, accident or health coverage available to a group — union members, a company's employees, etc. — under a single contract, usually without regard to the physical condition and age of the individuals insured.

Homeowners': Insures against damage to or loss of a residence, and its replacement; contents, personal property; loss from fire and theft, wind, flood; liability, etc.

Liability: Protects against financial loss from damage or injury to others for which the insured is legally liable, as in an auto, business, home, etc.

> *Umbrella Policy:* An extended liability coverage, usually greater than that of standard policies. There are personal and commercial umbrellas.

Life:

Annuity: Life insurance that guarantees fixed or variable payments to the policyholder (the *annuitant*) during the person's lifetime, or for a fixed number of years. Growth of capital in such policies is tax deferred.

Variable Annuity: Premiums are invested, at the direction of the annuitant, in securities and the annuitant receives payments based on the (variable) yield. Also called *variable life insurance.*

Refund Annuity: Provides a lump sum or installment payments to a beneficiary — on the death of the annuitant — for the amount remaining in the annuity.

Single Premium Annuity: A single payment covers the entire cost of the annuity. Popular for the deferred tax feature. Also called *single premium life insurance.*

Decreasing Term: Large life coverage for small premiums because the face value of the policy decreases while the premiums remain constant. Practical for young families with large responsibilities, but modest incomes. Decreasing term accumulates no cash value.

Endowment: Provides payment of a stated sum to the insured at the policy's maturity, or to a beneficiary, should the insured die before the maturity date.

Ordinary Life: Same as whole life.

Straight Life: Same as whole life.

Term: Premiums are paid over a limited time and insurance covers a specific term; the policy's face value is payable only if the insured dies within that term. Term builds no investment value, therefore it's inexpensive.

Whole Life: Premiums are paid throughout the insured's lifetime; cash value is built up (gains are tax-deferred) which can be borrowed against or withdrawn.

Convertible. A policy that can be converted to another type of policy without penalty, physical examination, etc.

Double-Indemnity. A life (or accident) insurance policy *clause* that provides for payment of twice the policy's face value in event of accidental death. Also called *accidental death benefit.*

> **"The meek shall inherit the earth, but not its mineral rights."**
> *John Paul Getty*

Mortgage: Coverage that makes mortgage payments, should the insured become disabled, and/or pays off the mortgage in the event of the insured's death.

Mutual: Insureds become *members* of the insurance company and mutually insure each other, paying premiums into a common fund, out of which losses are covered. A membership fee may be charged; surpluses may be returned to members as dividends or as reduced premium payments. See also: DIVIDEND

Renters': Like *homeowners',* without building coverage. (Used to be called *tenants'* insurance.)

Self: Instead of buying coverage from an underwriter, a business that is financially able may choose to insure itself against loss by establishing a special fund for the purpose: *self-insuring.*

Theft: Insures property against loss from theft.

Third Party: Insurance that pays for a loss — for which the insured is liable — to someone other than the insured.

....

▶ **Interest**

The amount a borrower pays to a lender for the use of his money, expressed as a percentage of the money borrowed for a stated time (usually one year).

Accrued Interest

Interest accumulated, but not yet paid out.

APR

Abbr.: **Annual (interest) Percentage Rate.** The actual percentage paid with interest, service charges, points, fees etc., calculated in; esp. home mortgages. Legally, the APR must be stated.

● **Compound Interest**

Interest paid on *both* the principal and on the interest it has *accrued*. Compounding may take place daily, quarterly, etc., as agreed (obviously, the more often, the more attractive the deal for the lender).

● **Simple Interest**

Interest payable on principal only, not compounded.

Interest Rate

The percentage of interest charged or paid. See also: MORTGAGE, POINTS

Prime Rate

The base lending rate charged by U.S. banks on business loans to their best large customers: higher than the FED's discount rate to the banks, lower than the banks' rate for consumer loans. See also: FED, DISCOUNT RATE

....

Interest Bearing Account

An account that pays interest on customers' deposited funds.

....

INTEREST RATES BANK, S&L ACCOUNTS

Interest rates for lowest minimum deposit. Larger deposits may earn higher rates.

	MMDAs	Super NOWs	6 mn. CD	1-yr. CD	2½ yr. CD	
Bank of America 6.15		4.00	8.25	8.25	8.00	†A
First Interstate Bank.......6.15		4.00	8.60	8.25	8.00	Au
Security Pacific Bank...4.75		4.00	8.40	8.40	8.20	c-B
Union Bank 6.15		4.00	8.65	8.65	8.55	Br
Wells Fargo Bank 6.15		4.00	8.25	8.25	8.00	
American S&L 5.50		5.25	9.20	9.10	N	
Citicorp Savings 6.25		4.00	8.80	8.80		
Great Western S		N	8.90,			
			9.25			

Money market deposit accounts *NOW accounts* *CDs of various maturities*

Chart is convenient to compare rates for different type savings accounts.

....

International(s)

Companies that have interests and do business in several countries. Also called *multinationals*.

....

International Fund   See: MUTUAL FUND

....

Inventory

A business' merchandise or stock on hand, available for sale, work-in-progress, raw materials and finished goods on hand, etc. Also, a complete list of these items.

....

Investment

An expenditure made in hope of a return, profit (as in the form of regular, steady income or an appreciation in value of the item invested in) over a period of time. See also: SAVING/INVESTMENT/SPECULATION section

Investment Analyst

One who researches and evaluates investments, partic-ularly corporate stocks and bonds. Analysts usually work with brokerage houses; the brokerages use analyses developed to assist clients and as sales tools.

Fundamental Analysis

Examination of a company's assets, management, cash, products, etc., to determine that company's real value. Good fundamental analysis may turn up hidden value not reflected in the stock's price.

Technical Analysis

Analysis of a market or a security by charting its performance and using historical patterns that appear on the charts in an attempt to predict direction: history repeats itself — maybe. A *chartist* does technical analysis.

Investment Bank(er)   See: BANK

Investment Strategy

A systematic plan by which investments are made.

....

Invoice

An itemized statement of goods shipped to a buyer, or of services rendered, stating quantities, prices, fees, shipping, terms, etc. (May also request payment.)

....

IPO   See: BUSINESS STRUCTURE
IRA   See: RETIREMENT PLAN

....

IRS

Abbr.:   **Internal Revenue Service**. The agency in the Department of Treasury responsible for collecting income taxes. See also TREASURY

....

Issue

A group or class of securities issued by a company. Also the *distribution* of the securities.

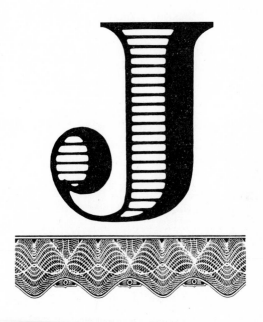

Joint Tenancy

Ownership of a property by two or more parties who share possession and interest equally. Upon the death of one, that party's share *automatically passes* to the remaining joint owner(s). A common form of husband/wife ownership. See also TENANCY IN COMMON

Joint Account

A bank, S&L, brokerage, etc., account held in the names of two people, each of whom can use it and have equal rights to it.

Joint Venture   See: BUSINESS STRUCTURE

Juggling the Books

Intentionally inaccurate bookkeeping — usually with the intent of covering theft or tax evasion.

....

Junk Bonds   See: BONDS
Junk Silver   See: METALS
Just Title   See: TITLE

*"A feast is made for laughter,
and wine maketh merry:
but money answereth all things."*
                                      Ecclesiastes

KEOGH See: RETIREMENT PLAN

Keynesian Economics

    The theories of English economist John Maynard Keynes, holding that full employment and a stable economy depend on continuing government stimulation of spending and investment by adjusting interest and tax rates, deficit spending, etc. Some attribute the U.S. national debt to the practice of Keynesian economics.

Kickback

    Giving back part of money received (as payment, commission, or fees) as a result of agreement or coercion. Ex.: an employee *kicking back* part of his salary as a condition of employment. Illegal.

Labor Union   See: UNION

Land   See: REAL ESTATE

....

Landlord

A person who owns land or buildings which are rented
to others.

....

Layoff

Temporary unemployment. Ex.: when a factory cuts back
production a layoff (of employees) may result.

....

Leading/Lagging Indicators   See: INDICATORS

....

Lease

A contract between a property owner (*lessor*) and another (*lessee*) to whom the right of possession and use of the property is transferred. The lease specifies time of possession, rent amount, date of payment, etc. See also RENT

Lease-Purchase (Agreement)

Lessee may apply lease payments made to the purchase price of the property (at a specified future time), and pay the difference between payments already made (or part of them) and the purchase price. *Rental-purchase* works the same way.

Sublease

A lease granted to another party by one who is already the lessee of a property; ex.: an apartment.

Leverage

Speculation in a business venture by using borrowed money, with the expectation of earning big profits. Also the *use* of such borrowed money.

Leveraged Buy-out, LBO   See: TAKEOVER

Liability

A legal obligation to pay for goods or services received, or to make good on loss or damage.

Liability, Accounting: Debt, accounts payable; obligations incurred but not paid. See also ASSET, INSURANCE

Libel

Any false and malicious written statement that exposes a person to public ridicule, humiliation or contempt which injures the person's reputation, and which may entitle the injured party to compensation for that injury.

Lien

A legal claim on the property of another as security for payment of a debt.

....

Life Insurance See: INSURANCE

Limited Partnership See: BUSINESS STRUCTURES

Limited Company — Ltd. See: BUSINESS STRUCTURES.

....

Line of Credit (Credit Line)

The maximum amount of credit that may be extended to a borrower, by a bank, etc. Such an arrangement gives the borrower flexibility in planning, and the use of credit only when needed.

....

Liquid(-ity)

Assets readily convertible into cash. Also the ability of a business to meet obligations without disposing of its fixed assets.

Liquid Asset

Cash or something convertible to cash. See also ASSET

....

Liquidate

To settle (liquidate) debts or accounts. Also, to *break up*, do away with; ex.: liquidate a business.

....

Listing

Stock Market: A company whose stock is included among those listed for trade on a stock exchange.

....

Living Will See: WILL

....

Load Fund   See: MUTUAL FUND

....

Loan

Granting temporary use of something, esp. money. Also
the act of lending.

Loan Value   See: INSURANCE

....

Lobby

A group that tries to influence legislation in favor of
a special interest. Also: *the act*. One who lobbies is
a *lobbyist*.

....

Locked In (Out) of a Market

If you own a security, commodity, etc., and want to sell it,
but there are *no buyers*, you're said to be locked in (to a
market). If there are *no sellers* when you want to buy,
you're locked out.

....

Long/Short Position

Being in a market as a buyer or seller.   Long: *buying* or
holding stocks, commodities, etc. — expecting the price
to rise. Ex.: a *long position* in wheat. Opposite is a *short
position*: *selling* something that one does not own, has
borrowed expecting its price to fall, so that delivery can
be made at a lower price.

....

Lot

A distinct portion of anything: land, securities, etc.

....

Lump Sum (Payment)
Debts paid in one (lump) sum.

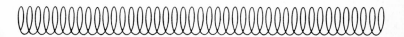

Majority (Minority) Interest

More than half of equity, shares, etc; less than half is a *minority interest.*

....

Malpractice

Improper or careless treatment of a patient or client by a professional, doctor, lawyer, etc., resulting in loss or injury.

Malpractice Insurance See: INSURANCE

Malpractice Suit

A lawsuit charging malpractice.

....

Managed Account

An account (securities, commodities, etc.) managed by a third party — hopefully a professional — instead of the account owner or his broker.

Management Fee

Fee charged for management services (of an account, a property, etc.)

....

Margin

Security (usually a percentage of a transaction) deposited by a client with a broker as a provision against loss on the transaction. The margin represents the client's investment or equity. Also the *act of depositing margin.* See also COMMODITIES

Margin Account

A brokerage house account which allows customers to buy securities *on margin* (on credit).

Margin Call

A brokerage demand on a margin account customer for more money, if the account balance falls below the percentage required. Also called a *house call.*

....

Market

A group carrying on extensive transactions (buying and selling) in a specific security or commodity. Also the *place;* ex.: a stock or commodity exchange.

Make a Market

Maintaining firm offers for a security, ready to buy or sell at prices quoted. Called a *market-maker* in the OTC market.

Market Letter   See: MONEY MEDIA appendix

Market Order

An order to buy or sell a specified amount of a stock, commodity, etc. at the best price available.

Market Value

The value of a business or property on the open market, what it can be sold for; current actual value.

....

Maturity

Due to be paid. The time when a note or bill becomes due.

....

Merchant Bank   See: BANK

Merger   See: BUSINESS STRUCTURES

....

Metals

A sector of the commodities market: copper, platinum, gold, silver, etc.   See also COMMODITIES

PRECIOUS METALS

Gold

Rare, easily formed but virtually indestructible yellow metal. Rarity, durability and beauty make it desirable and thus valuable. A traditional measure of value, often used to back national currencies. Also used for jewelry, ornamentation, coins and some industrial applications.

Goldbug

A person who believes (sometimes fanatically) in the wisdom of investing in gold. Also: *one who supports the gold standard*, esp. an economist or a politician.

Silver

White, ductile metal used for coins, jewelry, ornaments, mirrors, table utensils, photographic chemicals, conductors, etc. Also a backing for currency.

Junk Silver

U.S. coins minted before 1965 (when the government discontinued silver content in coins) that are badly worn, have no collectors' value and are sold by weight for silver content. Price is determined by silver's value per ounce at the time.

Platinum

Gray-white, heavy, malleable and ductile metal. Used
in chemical and scientific apparatus, catalytic converters
(platinum resists most chemicals and fuses only at high
temperatures) and expensive jewelry.

STRATEGIC METALS

Metals, such as *titanium,* etc. important for military applications. Strategic metals are not traded on the commodity markets; most trades are through specialized
brokers. Speculative, *extremely* high risk.

> *"Blessed are the young,
> for they shall inherit
> the national debt."*
> *Herbert Hoover*

Middleman

An intermediary; one who
plays an economic role
between producer and consumer.

Monetarism

The theory that changes in the *money supply* determine the
direction of a nation's economy. *Monetary policy:* a nation's policy toward managing its money supply. *Monetary unit:* the unit of value of a nation's currency; ex.: the
U.S. dollar, Swiss franc.

Money Supply

The sum of account deposits and the currency in circulation. The several measures of the money supply are
designated M-1, M-2, and M-3

Money

Anything used as a medium of exchange, a means of payment, or a measure of wealth.

Money Market

The market among financial institutions in safe, liquid short-term debt instruments: CDs, T-Bills, etc.

This self-explanatory chart lets you compare the money market rates available.

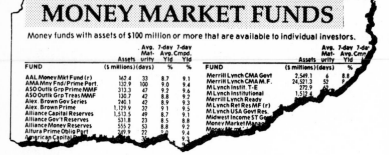

MONEY MARKET FUNDS

Money funds with assets of $100 million or more that are available to individual investors.

FUND	Assets ($ millions)	Avg. Mat- urity (days)	7-day Avg. Yld %	7-day Cmpd. Yld %	FUND	Assets ($ millions)	Avg. Mat- urity (days)	7-day Avg. Yld %
AAL Money Mkt Fund (r)	162.4	33	8.7	9.1	Merrill Lynch CMA Govt	2,549.1	6	8.8
AMA Mny Fnd/Prime Port.	132.9	100	9.0	9.4	Merrill Lynch CMA M.F.	24,521.3	52	P
ASO Outlk Grp Prime MMF	313.3	47	9.2	9.6	M Lynch Instit. T-E	272.9		
ASO Outlk Grp Treas MMF	130.7	42	8.8	9.2	M Lynch Institutional	1,512.4		
Alex. Brown Gov Series	240.1	42	8.9	9.3	Merrill Lynch Ready			
Alex. Brown Prime	1,129.9	32	9.1	9.5	M Lynch Ret Res MF (r)			
Alliance Capital Reserves	1,513.5	49	8.7	9.1	M Lynch USA Govt Res.			
Alliance Gov't Reserves	531.8	23	8.5	8.8	Midwest Income ST Go			
Alliance Money Reserves	555.2	53	8.8	9.2	Money Market Manag			
Altura Prime Oblig Port	249.9	22	9.0	9.4	Money Mk mt			
American Capital		36		9.3				

Monopoly

Exclusive control of a commodity or service in a market, or enough control to make manipulation of prices possible. Also, a group that has such control. See also ANTI-TRUST, CARTEL, TRUST

Moody's Investors Service

A securities rating service.

Moonlight

To work at an additional job after one's regular full-time employment, as at night. *Moonlighter*: the person; *moonlighting*: the act.

....

Moratorium

An authorized period of delay or waiting to make payment, to perform an obligation, to do something. Ex.: a community moratorium on building.

....

▶ Mortgage

A loan on real property, usually long term (15, 20, 30 years) with the property as security for the repayment of money borrowed. Also the *deed* which effects the transaction.

Foreclose

The reclaiming, by the lienholder, of a property from an owner who has defaulted on the mortgage on the property. Also the *act of foreclosing*.

Mortgage Insurance   See: INSURANCE

● TYPES OF MORTGAGES

Assumable Mortgage: May be passed from one borrower to another without changing lender or terms.

Chattel Mortgage: A lien against personal property: tools, equipment, etc.

First Mortgage: Has priority over other mortgages (second mortgage, etc.).

Fixed Rate Mortgage: Equal (fixed) monthly payments of principal and interest are paid over the life of the loan.

FHA Mortgage: Partially backed by the Federal Housing Authority, usually at an attractive interest rate.

Home Equity Mortgage: A loan using the equity homeowners have built up in their house as collateral.

MORTGAGE RATES

30-YEAR FIXED (BELOW $187,600)

Lender	Rate	Points	APR
Atlantic Financial	9.750	2.125	10.10
Phoenix Mortgage	9.750	2.500	10.24
J & J Mortgage	9.750	2.5	10
Western Heritage Financial			
United Funding			

Interest rate   *Points (percent of total) paid to get the loan*   *Annual Percentage Rate*

30-YEAR ADJUSTABLE (BELOW $187,600)

Lender	Rate	Points	Adj. period	Index	Margin	Caps	APR
J & J Mortgage	8.375	2.500	1 yr	1 yr T-Bill	2.750	2/6	11.10
Pacific Coast	8.500	2.000	6 mo	6 mo T-Bill	2.500	2/14	10.36
Pacific West Fin.	8.500	2.000	1 yr	1 yr T-Bill	2.7	2/5.5	
	8.625	2.00					

Adjustment period: how often the rate can be raised or lowered   *Security to which the rate is indexed*   *Difference between Index rate and the Mortgage rate*   *Lowest-highest rates that can be charged: the CAPS*

Price-level adjusted mortgage: Monthly payments vary with inflation rates instead of interest. *Abbr.:* **PLAM**.

Second Mortgage: The lien next in priority to a first mortgage.

Variable Rate Mortgage: Rate varies depending on some other rate (such as T-Bills). Monthly payments may vary, but there are maximums beyond which the rate cannot go: *caps*. Also called *adjustable rate mortgage*. *Abbr.:* **ARM**.

Wraparound Mortgage: Includes payments on a previous mortgage that's still in effect.

Multi-Family Dwelling   See: REAL ESTATE
Municipal Bond (Muni)   See: BOND

....

▶ **Mutual Fund**

Also called a *fund*. An investment company in which
investors buy shares; the company then invests the clients'
money in securities of the type in which the fund specializes. A *fund manager* directs investment activities and is
responsible for his fund's success. Any income or profit
from the investment, after expenses and fees, is pooled and
paid to the investors *proportionate* to their share of ownership. Funds issue shares continuously and are obligated to
redeem their shares on shareholders' demand, so liquidity
is high. Risk varies, depending on the type of fund.

Family of Funds

A company that offers a number of different types of
funds.

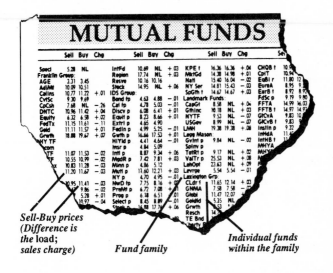

*Sell-Buy prices
(Difference is
the* load; *sales charge)*

Fund family

*Individual funds
within the family*

Load Funds

A mutual fund with sales charges, usually a percentage of the investment. Types of loads: 1) *Front-Load:* commission is charged when shares are sold to the customer; 2) *Back-Load*: charge is made when customers' shares are redeemed; 3) *Low-Load*: a low percentage service fee, either front or back; 4) *No-Load:* no sales commission or redemption fee is charged. (All funds charge yearly administrative fees.)

Telephone Switch (Transfer)

Many mutual funds allow customers to switch their money on account between funds the company offers, by telephone instruction. (*Written authorization* to phone switch is required.) Speed of transaction and investment flexibility make this a popular service; a per switch fee may be charged.

● TYPES OF FUNDS

Growth Funds: Objective is long-term gains by investing in companies with above-average earnings growth rates and high potential for capital growth.

Aggressive growth funds aim for maximum (capital) appreciation and may invest in fledgling companies, or be specialty funds, such as *international* or *sector funds* (see below).

Growth and Income Funds: Securities are bought in companies that combine earnings growth with rising dividends; these funds look for current income as well as long-term growth. They can invest in high-dividend stocks as well as fixed-income securities. The objective is a combination of investments that will gain capital appreciation while providing income.

Income Funds:

Money market funds. The goal of money market funds is safe current high income from short-term money market instruments. These funds offer stability, liquidity, and may even offer check-writing privileges and be tax-free.

Bond funds are of both taxable and tax-free varieties. *Investment-grade* bond funds seek high income from debt securities: corporate, government, municipal, tax-free bonds, etc. *High-yield* bond funds try for even higher income through *junk* (low-grade) debt.

International Funds:
Aim is aggressive capital growth from investments in companies outside of U.S. — along the Pacific Rim, in Europe, etc. Fund performance is subject to currency fluctuation and international political and economic considerations, as well as the (invested in) companies' business performances.

Sector Funds:
Are invested in businesses or groups of businesses in one specific business *sector,* electronics, health care, transportation, etc., and the goal is aggressive capital appreciation. Share price may be volatile.

(The above are general categories of funds. There are many funds in each category; most companies have coined their own names for the funds they offer — such as *Capital Growth*, *Cash Reserves*, etc. What the categories are called may also vary from company to company.)

....

Mutual Insurance   See: INSURANCE

National Debt

The financial obligations of a national government (owed to the nation's citizens and/or to other nations) resulting from deficit spending. Also called *public debt*.

....

Nationalize

To make national; esp. to bring under the control or ownership of a nation. Ex.: industries or land.

....

Negative Cash Flow   See: CASH FLOW

....

Negotiable (Securities)

Transferable by endorsement, if registered. Or by possession if not registered; title belongs to the one who has possession — a *bearer* instrument.

....

Next of Kin

A person's nearest blood relative(s).

....

Net Income/Loss

What's left after all deductions for taxes, charges, expenses, allowances, discounts and the like have been taken from a salary, business operation, etc.

....

Net Worth

Assets minus liabilities.

....

Newsletter, Market Letter   See: MONEY MEDIA appendix
No-Fault   See: INSURANCE

> *"Money doesn't always bring happiness. People with ten million dollars are no happier than people with nine million dollars."*   *Hobart Brown*

Nonprofit

Not for profit; the legal purpose and activities of tax-exempt entities such as churches, charities, hospitals or foundations.

....

Notary (Public)

One legally authorized to administer oaths and authenticate deeds and contracts.

....

Note

A written promise to pay an acknowledged debt, ex.: a promissory note. Also: a *negotiable* government or bank *certificate*.

New York Stock Exchange Composite Index

A group of stocks listed on the NYSE, added together and averaged for an indication of stock market performance. See also: STOCK (INDEX)

> *"Money is a fruit that is always ripe."*
> *English Proverb*

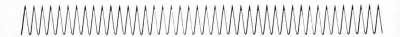

Odd Lot

Securities: A quantity less than a conventional trading unit (usually fewer than 100 shares). Also called *broken lot*.

Offer

A proposal or bid. *Offering price:* the sale price quoted. Esp. price per share of a security, mutual fund, etc. being sold to the public.

Off-Shore

Away from U.S shores; in a foreign country.

Off-shore Banking/Investment : Registered, located, conducted in a foreign country; outside the continental U.S., not subject to federal regulation (Cayman Islands, etc.). Ex.: an off-shore investment company, or bank.

Off-shore Oil: Platform exploration and drilling off-coast, in an ocean, gulf.

Operating Profit/Loss

The difference between a business' revenues and related costs and expenses, before income deductions. Also called *net operating profit/loss, operating income/loss, net operating income/loss.*

....

Option

The (purchased) right to buy or sell something (stock, etc.) within an agreed period of time, on specified terms, at a specified price. See also INSURANCE

Call (Option)

An option that gives you the right to *buy* a fixed amount of a specified stock, at a predetermined price, within a given time. (You'd buy a call option expecting the stock's price to go up.)

Put (Option)

An option giving the right to *sell* an amount of a stock at a fixed price within a fixed time period: bought by one expecting the stock's price to fall (opposite of *call*).

Stock Option   See: STOCK

....

Ordinary Life   See: INSURANCE

....

Over The Counter Market

Abbr.: **OTC.**   Stock of smaller, often younger, companies that do not qualify for NYSE or AMEX listings are sold over the counter. (There are many more OTC listings because there are more small companies.)

Quotes for stock traded OTC. Because there are so many OTC stocks, not all are listed and information is less detailed than NYSE or AMEX listings. (Bonds are also traded OTC.)

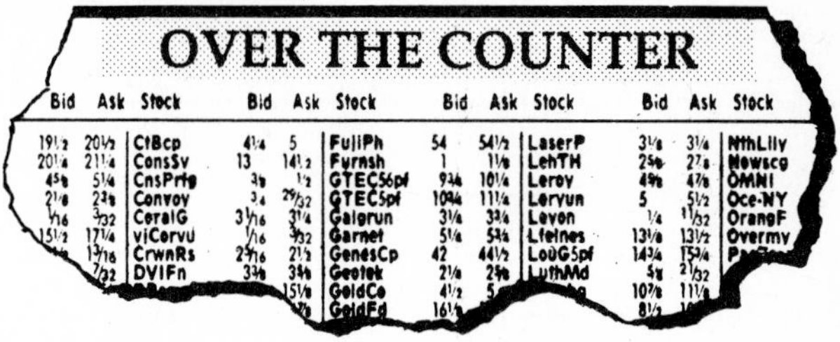

OVER THE COUNTER

Bid	Ask	Stock	Bid	Ask	Stock	Bid	Ask	Stock	Bid	Ask	Stock
19½	20½	CtBcp	4¼	5	FujiPh	54	54½	LaserP	3⅛	3¼	NthLily
20¼	21¼	ConsSv	13	14½	Furnsh	1	1⅛	LehTH	2⅝	2⅞	Newscg
4⅝	5¼	CnsPrtg	⅜	½	GTEC56pf	9¾	10¼	Leroy	4⅝	4⅞	OMNI
2⅛	2⅜	Convoy	¾	29/32	GTEC5pf	10¾	11¼	Leryun	5	5½	Oce-NY
1/16	3/32	CoralG	3 1/16	3¼	Galgrun	3⅛	3¾	Levon	¼	11/32	OrangF
15½	17¼	viCorvu	1/16	3/32	Garnet	5⅛	5¾	Lfelnes	13⅛	13½	Overmy
	1 3/16	CrwnRs	2 5/16	2½	GenesCp	42	44½	LouG5pf	14¾	15¾	
	7/32	DVIFn	3⅜	3⅝	Geotek	2⅛	2⅝	LuthMd	⅝	21/32	
				15⅛	GoldCo	4½	5		10⅞	11⅛	
				⅞	GoldFd	16½			8½		

Out-of-the-Market

Commodities: The price bid is unacceptably low.

Overhead

The general costs of running a business; overhead expenses, an overhead charge. The *fixed* business costs (utilities, rent, phone, etc.) which can't be charged against or attributed to a specific product or part of the work operation.

Overdraft

Overdrawing an account at a bank; a draft in excess of the balance in one's account. Also the *amount* of the excess.

Overdue

Past the promised time of payment; an overdue bill.

Overvalued

Valued too high; to put too high a price on stock, property, etc.

P/L

> *Abbr.:* **Profit and loss.** *Statement* of corporate profit
> or loss.

....

Pacific Rim

> Far Eastern markets/countries bordering the Pacific.

....

PSE

> *Abbr.:* **Pacific Stock Exchange.** West Coast equivalent
> of the NYSE in San Francisco.

....

Panic Selling

> Startling political or economic news can cause sudden,
> widespread financial concern which leads to heavy securi-
> ties selling — at any price. There's a panic to get into cash
> and out of the markets before they drop further. See also
> CRASH OF '29, BLACK MONDAY

....

Paper Profit

When something owned goes up in value, no real profit is realized until it's sold: profit is just on paper.

....

Par Value

A business' shares that may be purchased at the original price (*issue par*), or at *face value* (*nominal par*).

....

Partnership   See: BUSINESS STRUCTURES

....

Passbook

A bankbook; a small book that's each depositor's private ledger.

Passbook Savings Account

A savings account where transactions are entered into the account holder's passbook. Usually a safe, low-risk account that pays low interest.

> *"I don't like money, actually, but it quiets my nerves."*
> *Joe Louis*

Past Due

Overdue; the bill is past due. Overdue business payments or receipts: *past dues*.

....

Payables

Amounts owed to creditors for goods and services: a business' liabilities.   See also ACCOUNTS PAYABLE/RECEIVABLE

....

Payout

Paying or disbursing money. Ex.: a dividend.

....

Payroll Tax Deduction   See: TAX
P/E (Price-Earnings Ratio)   See: STOCK

....

Penalty

Punishment for violating laws, rules, esp., for late payment or non-payment of taxes. Also, *something forfeited* for violating the terms of an agreement.

....

Penny Stocks   See: STOCK

....

Pension

Fixed amount paid at regular intervals to a person (or their survivors) in consideration of past services, age, etc. Esp.: a retirement or disability pension.

Pension Fund

Fund to provide members benefits under a pension plan. (Pension funds are large *institutional investors*.)

Pension Plan

A contributory or noncontributory plan created and maintained by a corporation, union, government, etc., to provide pensions for participants.

An employee becomes *vested* when he has the legal right to a plan's full benefits. (Employees' contributions to plans are always their property, regardless of whether they eventually qualify for full benefits.)
See also VESTED

....

Perk

An incentive; *perks* are offered to executives to encourage above average job performance.

Petrodollars

Surplus dollars accumulated by petroleum exporting countries (esp. as used for foreign investment and loans).

PIK

Abbr.: **Payment in kind.** Esp.: securities, where interest or dividends due is paid in additional securities instead of cash. See also: FUNNY MONEY

Pit

The commodity exchange floor area where trading in a specific commodity takes place. Ex.: the *corn pit.*

> *"Money is what you'd get on beautifully without if only other people weren't so crazy about it."* — Margaret Case Harriman

PLAM See: MORTGAGE

Platinum See: METALS

Point(s)

Basis Point: One hundredth of one percent — of interest rates, yields, etc.

Point, Finance: A price quotation unit. One dollar in stock transactions, one hundredth of a cent in cotton, one cent in pork, etc. Ex.: the price dropped a point.

Point, Real Estate: One percent of the value of a (mortgage) loan. Points may be added on as a service charge or fee for getting a loan; paid in advance or at closing. See also APR, INTEREST

....

Poison Pill   See: TAKEOVER

....

Point-of-Sale (-Purchase)

A retail store; also: *check-out* counter in the store.

> ## "If you make money your god, it will plague you like the devil."
> *Henry Fielding*

Policy   See: INSURANCE

....

Portfolio

Finance: An individual's or an institution's total investment holdings: stock, commodities, property, etc.

....

Position

When one owns a security or commodity, one is said to have a position in a market. See also COMMODITIES, LONG/SHORT POSITION, STOCK

....

Postal Savings Bank   See: BANK

Power of Attorney

A document in which one person authorizes another to act as agent on behalf of the principal (signer). A power of attorney must be notarized, may authorize full or limited power, and becomes void should the signer die.

Precious Metal   See: METALS

Predator

A person or company that attempts the hostile takeover of a corporation.

Preferred Stock   See: STOCK

Premium

Finance: A sum, additional to interest, paid to get a loan.

Insurance: A fee paid for insurance coverage.

Securities: Amount by which a security sells above its *par* value.

Prepay(ment)

To pay before due, esp., a mortgage.   See also MORTGAGE

Prepayment Penalty

A penalty for early repayment of a loan or mortgage.

Presale

A sale before an advertised sale (for select customers).

Presell

   To sell in advance of manufacture or construction.

....

Pretax   See: TAX

....

Price

   Amount paid for something offered for sale.

   Price Control: Regulation of prices by a government.
   Ex.: rent control.

   Price Cut(ting): Selling something below its usual price.

   Price Fluctuation: Changes in price, esp. investments.

   Price Fixing: Establishing the price of something at a
   predetermined level by government or by mutual agreement
   among sellers or producers. Ex.: OPEC (attempts) *fixing*
   oil's price.

   Price Support: Maintaining a commodity's price, esp. by
   government subsidy or by its purchase of surpluses.

....

**Prime, Prime Interest Rate, Prime Lending Rate, Prime
Rate** See: INTEREST

....

Principal

   Finance: Capital, as distinguished from interest, profit.
   See also CAPITAL

....

Private/Public Company   See: BUSINESS STRUCTURES

....

Probate

   Law: To establish authenticity or validity. Esp. of a will in
   a probate court, when an administrator is appointed to carry
   out the will's instructions.

....

> *"The only thing I like about rich people is their money."*
> **Lady Astor**

Profit

Gain from capital or property invested. See also CAPITAL

Gross Profit

Gross (total) receipts, minus cost of goods, but *before* deduction of other costs, e.g., rent, salaries, etc.

Net Profit

Profit after all costs have been deducted.

Profit Sharing

Sharing of profits; ex.: additional to wages, employees receive a share of a business' profits as an incentive.

Profit-Taking

Selling securities after price rises above costs in order to take a profit.

Profiteer

One who seeks exorbitant profit, esp. through sale of scarce goods. Also the act: *profiteering*.

Programmed Trading

Trading of securities by computer. Software programs express the trader's trading criteria and automatically initiate trades when the criteria are met.

Programmed trading was a culprit in the market's 500+ point crash in October 1987— Black Monday. The trading volume jammed the electronic systems, and investors lost billions, which led to tighter SEC control of the practice. See also BLACK MONDAY, BLOCK TRADING, INSTITUTIONAL TRADING

Promissory Note See: NOTE

Property

Personal Property

Cars, boats, furniture, etc. Nearly anything of worth an individual owns.

Real Property

Real estate.

Proprietor (-ship) See: BUSINESS STRUCTURES

Prorate

To divide or distribute, proportionately; ex.: expenses.

Pro Forma

Documentation provided in advance of shipment, showing only the description and quantity of goods shipped, but no terms of payment; ex.: a pro forma invoice.

Prospect

A prospective customer.

Prospectus

Brochure describing features, benefits of a business, place, etc. to potential clients. (By law, stock prospectus must be made available to potential buyers.)

Protectionism (-ist)

Protecting domestic industries from foreign competition by placing duties or quotas on imports. See also: TARIFFS

Proxy

Authorization by one person for another to act as the former's representative. Also: *written authorization* (power of attorney) empowering a person to act or vote for the signer — as at a stockholders' meeting.

Public Utility

Business enterprises performing essential public services: power, gas, sewer, etc. Utilities are regulated by federal, state and/or local governments.

Utilities

Public utility companies' stocks or bonds.

Purchasing Power

The ability to buy goods; the value of money for buying goods now, compared to what it used to buy. Also called *buying power*.

Put   See: OPTION

Pyramid Selling

A scheme in which people are enticed through promotions to buy — and to recruit others to buy — at a (seemingly) low price, a product that (supposedly) can be resold at a higher price for quick profit. The scheme works only if later buyers pay more than did the initial buyers; the practice may be illegal.

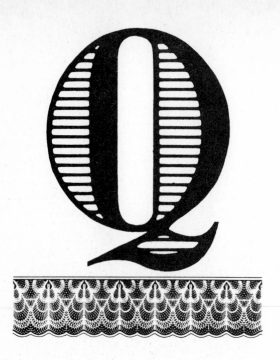

Quarter

One fourth of a fiscal year.

....

Quarterly Payments

Payments made at quarterly intervals; ex.: taxes, dividends, insurance.

....

Quarterly Report

Quarterly performance update sent by a corporation to its stockholders. See also ANNUAL REPORT

Quarterly Results

Performance for a quarter: contents of quarterly report.

....

> *"It doesn't matter if you're rich or poor, as long as you've got money."*
>
> *Joe E. Lewis*

Quota

An allotment; a limited amount (imports, immigration, etc.).

....

Quote (-ation)

Statement of the current price of a commodity or security.
Also the price quoted.

Rally

Securities: A sharp price rise, following an earlier decline; increased activity, after a slow period, by traders forming the stock market.

Ranch   See: REAL ESTATE

Random Walk

Theory that securities and commodity prices react to information coming into the markets in a random fashion, and that price history and fundamental analysis are of little use for forecasting a market's future direction.

Reaganomics

Economic policies put forth by the administration of President Ronald Reagan. See also: SUPPLY-SIDE ECONOMICS, TRICKLE-DOWN THEORY

....

Real Estate

Property, esp. land. Over the years, real estate has generally proven a sound investment — a roof over your head is nearly always a sound investment. Like other hard assets, successful real estate investment requires buying at the right price (and at the right time and place) and finding a buyer if you want to sell.

Real property: An estate of property — land, buildings, improvements attached to the land, mineral rights, etc.

Realty: Real estate or real property.

Closing

The meeting at which procedures are carried out to execute a sales contract.

Closing Costs

Fees charged to a purchaser by a bank, lawyer, etc., for services related to a sale — as a title search, appraisal, etc. Also any *expense additional* to the purchase price of a house, land, etc., paid by buyer or seller at the completion of the sale.

Realtor

One who works in the real estate business, belongs to the National Association of Real Estate Boards (and presumably follows their code of ethics).

Zoned

Refers to the division of a city, town, etc., into areas in which building style and/or activities are restricted. Ex.: residential, commercial, industrial zones, etc.

● **TYPES OF REAL ESTATE**

Apartment: A room or suite of rooms — usually rented — for living quarters; esp. one suite in an apartment house.

Apartment House (Complex): A building or group of buildings made up of a number of apartments. Also called a multi-family dwelling. *Flat:* An apartment that's all on one level. A *high-rise* is a building with a number of stories, equipped with elevators; ex.: a high-rise apartment building. *Mother-in-law apartment:* An apartment, usually small, often converted from existing vacant space in what otherwise would be a single-family house. *Tenement (house):* A rundown, often overcrowded apartment house, esp. in a poor section of a large city.

Condominium (Condo): Essentially, an apartment that is *owned* instead of rented. Fees, based on space proportionate to the total, are paid to a condo association to manage and maintain the building and common areas and services. Each owner receives a recordable deed with rights to sell, mortgage, remodel, etc., his unit. Also the individually owned units of an apartment house, office building or other multiple-unit complex. *Co-operative:* Similar to a condominium, but the owners take a direct role in the management of the property. *Duplex, Triplex, etc.-plex:* A two-, three- or more-unit apartment or condo building.

Commercial Real Estate: Office buildings, warehouses, factories used by companies for manufacturing, trade, business.

Income Property: Property that generates income through rent; usually refers to residential rentals.

Land: An area of earth surface, minerals beneath it, natural growth upon it, buildings and fences attached to it, air space rights (to a certain height) above it.

Farm: A tract of land, usually with a house, barn, fences, etc., on which crops and/or livestock are raised for a livelihood. *Truck Farm:* A farm growing vegetables or fruit for market. Also called a *truck garden.*
Ranch: A land operation for raising livestock under range conditions; also a large farm used primarily to raise one kind of crop or animal.

> *"Never invest your money in anything that eats or needs repairing."*
> **Billy Rose**

Residence: A place, esp. the house, in which a person lives or resides — dwelling place, home. *Residential real estate:* Houses, apartments, etc.

Single-Family Dwelling: A free-standing house where one family resides. *Rowhouse:* One of a row of houses having nearly uniform plans and architectural treatment, as in certain housing developments; a house having at least one side wall in common with a neighboring dwelling. A *townhouse* also has similar characteristics.

Second Home: An additional residence — in the country, the mountains or on the coast — where owners go on weekends, vacations, etc. Also a *vacation home.*
Timeshare: A plan in which several people share ownership or rental costs of a vacation home, condo, etc., which entitles each to a certain amount of use-time each year.

Shopping Center: A group of stores clustered together, esp. in suburban areas. Also a *shopping mall* or *plaza*. *Strip Shopping Center:* A small shopping center with shops side by side along a street or secondary road.

Starter Home: A first house, usually inexpensive, used to build equity. May also be a *fixer-upper:* needs work by the new owner.

> **"The safest way to double your money is to fold it over once and put it in your pocket."**   *Frank McKinney Hubbard*

Real Income

The amount of goods and services that income adjusted for inflation will buy.

....

Rebate

A partial refund; to return part of a payment for goods.

....

Receipt

Written acknowledgement of having received money, goods, etc., and of the amount.

....

Receivable(s)

Account(s) awaiting receipt of payment. See also:
ACCOUNTS PAYABLE/RECEIVABLE

Recession

A downturn in a country's economy, as measured by a
decline in GNP for two consecutive quarters. An upturn
in the economy, following a recession, is a *recovery.*

Redeem

To *pay off;* to clear (a debt) by payment. To pay off
something mortgaged. To *exchange* bonds, etc. for cash.

Red Ink

A deficit, a business loss — *in the red;* opposite: *black ink.*

Redlining

The practice of marking off areas as ineligible for credit,
because of race or economic status.

Refinance

To change the financing of a home, business, etc. by getting
additional credit, selling stock, etc., usually on new terms.
A practice often associated with real estate.
Recapitalization is a change in a corporation's capital
structure. See also: FINANCE

Refund Annuity   See: INSURANCE

Registered Bond   See: BOND

Rent

Periodic payments made by a tenant to a landlord for the use of an apartment, land, a building or an office, etc. *Rental* is the amount paid or received as rent. A *renter* is one who rents, controls a property through rent payment.

Rent Control

Control by a municipality over rent charged within its borders for housing; such property is *rent-controlled*. A *rent board* is a body that oversees and polices rent control policies, and hears renters' problems and complaints.

Renter's Credit

A tax credit some renters may be entitled to.

Rent Strike

A temporary, organized refusal by tenants of a building (apartment house) to pay their rent, as in protest over inadequate maintenance/services.

Tenant

A person or group that rents and occupies land, a house, an office, etc. from another. *Tenant Farmer:* a farmer who farms the land of another and pays rent in cash or with a part of the crops grown.

"I'd like to live like a poor man with lots of money."
Pablo Picasso

Resale

The act of selling a second time; second-hand, used.

Resale License: Allows a buyer to buy products which are to be resold, without paying sales tax. The *last* seller then collects the tax from the final user, avoiding duplication of tax charged.

> *"Waste of public money is like the sin against the Holy Ghost."*
> **Viscount Morley**

Reserves

Something kept back to use in the future (cash, oil, etc.).

Reserves, Finance: Cash, or assets readily convertible into cash, held aside — by a corporation, bank, state or national government, etc. — to meet expected or unexpected demands.

Reserves, Law: Uninvested cash kept available to comply with legal requirements.

....

Reserve Bank See: BANK

Residence See: REAL ESTATE

....

Resource

A source of supply, support or aid, esp. one held in reserve. Something a country, state, corporation, etc., has and can use to advantage. Ex.: financial resources, human resources, natural resources.

....

Resume

A brief written account or summary of personal, educational, and professional qualifications and experience, such as that a job applicant prepares.

Retail

Sale of goods to ultimate consumers at (full) *retail price*.

Retained Earnings

A corporation's accumulated — but undistributed — earnings. Also called *retained income, earned surplus*.

▶ Retirement Plans

Systematic savings plans to provide for individual future retirement.

Defined Benefit

High income individuals may shelter a limited part of their income in a defined benefit retirement plan. (May be appropriate for self-employed, older people.) Administrative costs for these plans are high compared to other plans, because of additional actuarial work required.

IRA

Abbr.: **Individual Retirement Account.** Exactly what the name says. For those not covered by another (company, etc.) plan, a limited amount of earned income may be saved each year on a tax deductible basis in an IRA (in a mutual fund, savings plan, etc.), with tax on that money and its earnings being *deferred* until retirement. At that time, presumably, the saver's income and the related tax obligation will be lower.

Spousal IRA

The IRA of an employed spouse who is not covered by another retirement plan.

> *"When I was young I thought that money was the most important thing in life; now that I am old I know that it is."*
>
> *Oscar Wilde*

KEOGH Plan

A tax-deferred retirement plan for self-employed individuals and small businesses. Named for Brooklyn Congressman Eugene J. Keogh, the chief sponsor of the legislation establishing the plan. It allows a *percentage* of income to be put into the plan with *tax deferred* 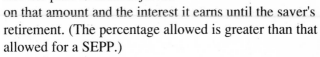 on that amount and the interest it earns until the saver's retirement. (The percentage allowed is greater than that allowed for a SEPP.)

An employer who has a KEOGH for himself is obligated to offer the same program to qualified employees — after a specified period of employment — and to participate in contributions to the plan on their behalf.

SEPP

Abbr.: **Simplified Employee Pension Plan.** Another plan — also *tax deferred* — for the self-employed or small business person. Similar to a KEOGH but with administrative differences.

There is usually a (annual) fee charged by the managing institution to administer IRA, KEOGH and SEPP accounts.

Some company pension plans may be *rolled-over* into these accounts to take advantage of the tax benefits. The plans' withdrawal age is 59½ years, earliest; there are *severe penalties* for early withdrawal: full payment of all taxes deferred, plus a substantial fine. (Withdrawals *must* begin by age 70.) See also: PENSION PLAN, ROLL-OVER

Return

Yield or profit (on investment), as from labor, land, business, stock, bonds, etc.

Tax Return: A statement on official forms of income, deductions, exemptions, etc., and taxes due. Also the *form*.

Revenue

Government: Income from taxation, excise duties, customs, or other sources, collected to pay public expenses.

Investment: The return or yield from any kind of patent, property, service, etc.: income. Money regularly coming in.

Revenue Agent

A government official responsible for collecting revenue. Also called a *revenuer* (obsolete).

Revenue Bond   See: BOND

Revenue Sharing

The disbursal of part of federal tax revenues to state and local governments for their use.

Revenue Stamp

A stamp showing that a government tax has been paid.

Revenue Tariff

A tariff or duty imposed on imports, primarily to produce public revenue.

Revolving Credit

Credit automatically available up to a predetermined limit (*credit line* or *line of credit*), while periodic payments are made. Also called a *revolving charge account.*

Rider

An addition or an amendment to a document. See also: INSURANCE

Right-to-Know

Laws or policies that make government or company data and records available to the individuals concerned.

Right-to-Work   See: UNION

Risk

Insurance: Exposure to the possibility of injury or loss. The *degree of probability* of such loss; also the *amount* that might be lost.

Business: Any possibility of loss because of price, demand, material availability, etc.

Risk Capital   See: VENTURE CAPITAL

Take (or Run) a Risk

To expose oneself to the chance of injury or loss; put oneself in danger — venture.

Risk Management

A technique (also, a *profession*) of assessing, minimizing and preventing accidental loss to a business, as through safety measures, insurance, etc.

Risk-Taker

A person or corporation inclined to take greater than average risks.

Risk Arbitrage   See: ARBITRAGE

Rollback

A return to a lower level of prices, wages, etc., as by government order.

Rollover

Renegotiate — as a loan or mortgage rate; new terms — after a period of time or under specified conditions. Also the *reinvestment* of retirement accounts in a plan to defer taxes. See also: RETIREMENT PLANS

Rowhouse   See: REAL ESTATE

Royalty

Compensation or a portion of the proceeds paid to the owner of a right — as a patent or oil or mineral right — for its use. An agreed portion of the income from a work paid to its author, composer, etc.; usually a percentage of the retail price of each copy sold.

Runner

A messenger of a bank or brokerage house. A person whose business it is to solicit patronage or trade. A collector, agent or the like for a bank, broker, etc.

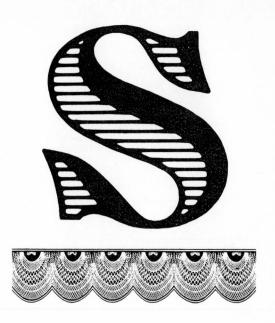

Safe Deposit Box

A lockable metal box or drawer, esp. in a bank vault, used for safely storing valuables — documents, jewelry, etc.

....

Sales Tax   See: TAX

....

Sallie Mae

Securities backed by low-cost loans for education, made to qualified students through the government chartered private company, the *Student Loan Marketing Association*; *abbr.:* **SLMA**

....

> ## *"I've got all the money I'll ever need if I die by four o'clock."*
> *Henny Youngman*

▶ **Save**

To set aside a reserve:
to save money.

Savings: That which is saved.

Savings Account: an interest-
paying bank account;
a passbook account.

Savings Certificate: a certificate
of deposit for a specific sum
of money in a savings account,
esp. a deposit for a fixed term at a specified interest rate.
Also called a *certificate of deposit; Abbr.:* **CD**.

Savings Bank See: BANK

Savings Bond See: TREASURY

....

S&L

Abbr.: **Savings and loan association**.   A government
chartered and regulated savings institution that takes
customers' deposits in exchange for ownership shares;
funds are primarily invested in loans secured by first
mortgages on homes. Recently, hundreds of S&Ls have
failed, requiring a massive federal bail-out. Also called
building and loan.

....

SBA

Abbr.: **Small Business Administration.**   Government
agency that provides financial and management assistance
to small or minority businesses that may lack the expertise,
credit, etc. to be completely competitive.

Seat

Right to membership privileges in a (stock) exchange.
Seats on an exchange are bought and sold.

SEC

Abbr.: **Securities and Exchange Commission.**   A five
member government board charged with regulating the
public offer and sale of securities, by seeing that the public
is informed and that securities are not misrepresented.
Created by the *Securities Exchange Act.*

Second Mortgage   See: MORTGAGE

Second Home   See: REAL ESTATE

Sector

A distinct part, esp. of society or of a nation's economy.

Sector Fund   See: MUTUAL FUND

Securities

Evidence of debt, as a bond.

Securities Analyst   See: INVESTMENT ANALYST

Seed Money

Capital for the start-up stages of a new business, esp.
for early operating costs. See also: VENTURE CAPITAL

Self Employed

Working for oneself — a professional, freelancer, consultant, etc.— rather than as a wage earning employee.

....

Self Insurance   See: INSURANCE

....

Seller Liability

A seller's *obligation* to disclose a product's (car, house, etc.) faults to its buyer, or be liable for correcting those faults after the sale. Now a law in some states.

....

Sellers' Market   See: BUYERS' MARKET

....

Sell-Off

A sudden drop in securities' prices as a result of widespread selling. Also the liquidating of assets, subsidiaries, etc.

....

Selling Short

Stock, Commodities: To sell a stock, etc. without having possession of it at the time of sale; the seller expects the (sold) item's price to drop, so the item can be bought cheaper for delivery, thus providing a profit. Such a seller has a *short position* (in the market). The opposite is taking a *long position* — buying and expecting the price to rise for a profit. *Short sale*: the act. *Short seller:* a speculator who sells short; the account is a *short account*. See also: LONG/SHORT POSITION

Short Covering

Buying securities or commodities *to replace* those a short seller *borrowed* to sell short.

> ***"Money often costs too much."***
> *Ralph Waldo Emerson*

Short Interest
Total amount of securities sold short, and not repurchased to cover *short positions*. Reported monthly; an indication of traders' optimism — or pessimism.

....

Semi-Durable Goods
Clothing, furniture, etc. — goods that are neither perishable nor lasting. Also called semi-durables.

....

Senior Citizen
An elderly or retired person, esp. one whose principal income is a pension or Social Security benefits.

....

Seniority
Priority or status gained by length of service (as in a profession, company, or union).

....

SEPP   See: RETIREMENT PLANS

....

Service Business
A business that sells services as opposed to manufactured products. A *service economy* refers to the economy of a country whose primary product is services.

....

Service Charge

A fee charged for a service, sometimes in addition to a basic charge. Ex.: a bank charge on a checking account when the balance averages below a specified minimum.

Share

One of the equal fractional parts into which the capital stock of a company or corporation is divided. An owner of shares is a *shareholder*. See also: STOCK

Sick Pay

Compensation paid by an employer to an employee who is absent from work because of illness. The absence is called *sick leave*.

Sight Draft

A draft (a check, etc.) payable (by a bank, etc.) upon its presentation.

Signature Loan

A loan requiring no collateral; an unsecured loan.

Silent Partner See: BUSINESS STRUCTURES
Silver See: METALS

Silver Certificate

A U.S. paper currency (now obsolete) redeemable for silver.

Silver Standard

A monetary standard or system using silver of specified weight and fineness to define the basic unit of currency.

Silver Thursday

> March 27, 1980 — the day Texas' Hunt brothers missed a hundred million dollar margin call on their silver contracts — which sent the silver market into a dive.

Simple Interest See: INTEREST
Single-Premium See: INSURANCE

SLIC

> *Abbr.:* **Savings and Loan Insurance Corporation.**
> Insures customer's deposits in S&Ls.

Slumlord

> A landlord who owns slum buildings; esp. one who fails to maintain his property and charges exorbitant rents.

Slushfund

> Money used for illegal or corrupt political purposes, such as for buying influence.

"Most of us hate to see a poor loser —or a rich winner."
Harold Coffin

Small Investor

> Investors (individually or as a group) who invest on their own behalf.

Socialism

A social theory or system that advocates community ownership and control of production, the distribution of capital,
land, etc. An advocate of socialism is a *socialist*.

Socialized Medicine

A system to provide a country's entire population with
medical care through government subsidy and control
of medical and health services.

Social Security

A government program of old age, unemployment, health,
disability and survivors' insurance maintained through
compulsory contributions by employers and employees.
Administered by the *Social Security Administration*;
abbr: **SSA**.

Social Security Act

Law establishing old age retirement insurance, a federal/
state program of unemployment compensation and federal
grants for state welfare programs.

Sole Proprietor   See: BUSINESS STRUCTURES

Solvent

Able to pay all just debts. Also: *solvency* — the condition
of being solvent; *insolvency* is the opposite.

Special Checking Account

A checking account that requires no minimum balance, but
on which a small charge is made for monthly maintenance,
as well as for each check issued or drawn on the account.

Speculation

Engaging in high-risk business transactions that offer
the potential for large gains or losses. Esp. trading
commodities, stocks, etc., hoping to profit from price
changes. Also: *to speculate* — the act; *speculator* —
the person.

....

Spin-Off See: BUSINESS STRUCTURES
Split See: STOCK

....

Spot Market

A market in which
commodities such as
grain, gold or crude
oil are bought and sold
for cash and immediate
delivery — on the spot,
as distinguished from
the futures market.
Spot price: An item's
price on the spot market.
Also called the *cash market*.

....

*Commodity cash prices
on the Spot Market*

SPOT PRICES

Nonferrous metal prices Tuesday
Aluminum $1.0100 per pound, NY Comex
spot month closed Tue.
Copper - $1.5170 a pound, U.S. destina-
tions.
Copper - 148.80 cents per pound, NY
Comex spot month Tue.
Lead - 39½-42 cents a pound.
Zinc - 72 cents a pound, delivered
Tin - $4.6034 Metals Week c
price per lb.)
Gold - $418.40 Handy &
daily quote).
London Gold - $419.65 p
$2.90.
Silver - $6.095 Handy
daily quote).
Silver - $6.061 per tro
spot month closed Tue.
Mercury - $285.00-$310
New York
Platinum
(contract
Pl

Spread

The difference between the price bid and the price asked for
a stock or a commodity, for a given time; a type of *straddle*
in which the *call price* is placed above and the *put price* is
placed below the current market quotation. See also:
HEDGING, OPTION, STRADDLE

....

Spreadsheet

Accounting: A work sheet arranged in a mathematical matrix and containing a multicolumn analysis of related entries on a single sheet for easy reference. May be an *electronic* spreadsheet.

Spousal IRA   See: RETIREMENT PLANS

Stagflation

An inflationary period accompanied by rising unemployment and lack of growth in consumer demand and business activity: *stagnant + inflation.*

Stamps   See: COLLECTIBLE
Stamp Tax   See: TAX

Standard Money

Money made of metal, with utility and value beyond its use for monetary exchange; ex: gold coins — *gold standard.*

Standard of Living

The level of everyday subsistence and comfort experienced by an individual, group, nation.

Standard & Poors 500 Stock Index

Called the S&P 500. While not so often quoted as the Dow, the S&P 500 may be more representative of the market's performance because of the greater number of stocks considered. See also: STOCK

Standard & Poors Rating

Security quality ratings made by Standard and Poors Corp.

> *"A nickel goes a long way now.*
> *You can carry it around for days*
> *without finding a thing it will buy."*
> *Anonymous*

State Aid
Financial support given by
a state government to a local
institution that serves the public;
ex.: a school, library.

....

State Bank   See: BANK

....

Statement
An abstract of an account showing the balance of assets and
liabilities.

Statement Savings Account
A bank account in which transactions are periodically
confirmed by a statement.

....

Stipend
Fixed or regular pay; salary. Esp. a scholarship or
fellowship allowance granted to a student.

....

▶ Stock
Business: A supply of goods kept on hand for sale to
customers by a merchant, manufacturer, etc.: inventory.
Finance: The outstanding capital of a corporation. Stock
investments represent equity and have high liquidity;
risk varies, dependent on the individual stock. Also called
shares (of a corporation).

Blue Chip Stock

Stock of strong, old line companies — ATT, IBM, GM, etc.

● Common Stock

Ownership units of a corporate business. Common Stock has voting rights and is entitled to dividends (after preferred stock). See also CAPITAL STOCK, DIVIDEND, PREFERRED STOCK

P/E

Abbr.: **Price-Earnings Ratio**.   Price of a share of common stock divided by its per-share earnings over the period of a year. A 10:1 ratio means the stock could earn its price back in ten years; a 100:1 would take a century.

Penny Stock

Very low-priced, extremely high risk speculative stock.

● Preferred Stock

Stock that has a superior claim (over common stock) to dividends — and perhaps to assets, should the company be liquidated. Dividends are paid at a fixed rate, regardless of the issuing corporation's performance. Preferred stock doesn't have voting privileges.

Convertible stock

Preferred stock that can be converted to common stock.

Secondary Issues

Stock: Almost as attractive as *blue-chip* but not quite.

Stockbroker   See: BROKER

Stock Certificate

A certificate evidencing ownership of corporate stock.

Stock Company

A company or corporation, the capital of which is divided into shares represented by stock.

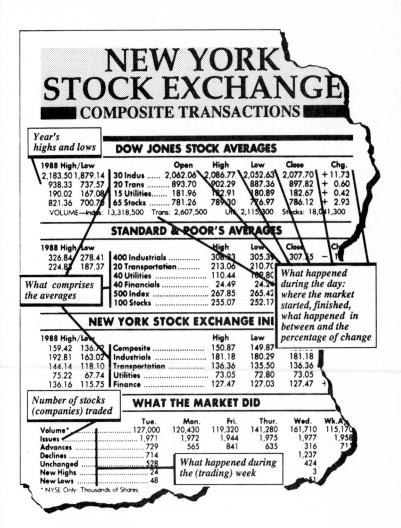

Stock Exchange

A place where securities are bought and sold; an association of brokers and dealers in stocks and bonds who transact business according to fixed rules.
Also called the *stock market*. There are more than 140 exchanges worldwide: in Frankfurt, Hong Kong, London, NYC, San Francisco, Tokyo, Zurich, etc.

Stockholder

One who owns at least one share of a corporation's stock.
Also called a *shareholder*.

Stockholders' Equity

The net assets of a corporation as owned by stockholders
in capital stock, capital surplus and undistributed earnings.

Stock Index

A group of stocks listed together, weighted and measured
by total performance.
Stock Indexes: Dow-Jones Stock Averages; Standard &
Poors 500 Stock Index; NY Stock Exchange Composite
Index; Nikkei Average, Tokyo; Financial Times — Stock
Exchange 100-Share Index (nick-named *Footsie* by
traders), in London etc.

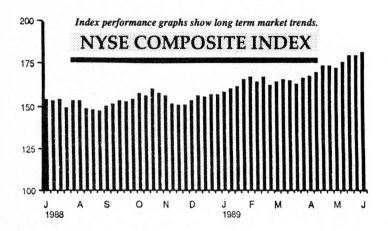

Index performance graphs show long term market trends.
NYSE COMPOSITE INDEX

Stock Ledger

A permanent record of the capital stock of a corporation,
listing stockholders' names and addresses, the number
of shares owned, and the serial numbers of their stock
certificates.

Stock Market

Refers to organized securities trading — stocks and bonds. *Blue Chip stock* of old, secure companies, *secondary issues* of companies only slightly less attractive, *growth stock* of young fledgling companies, and very high risk speculative *penny stock* make up the actual *stock* market. See also: MARKET, OTC, STOCK EXCHANGE

"Anyone who thinks there's safety in numbers hasn't looked at the stock market pages."
Irene Peter

Stock Option

A privilege (often set by an employment contract) giving the holder (usually an officer or employee) the right to buy stock of the issuing corporation at a specific price, within a stated period of time.

Stock Offer

Offer of a corporation's stock for sale. A company's first offer is its *initial public offer*. *Abbr.:* **IPO**.

Stock Split

A high priced stock that's awkward to sell may be divided — *split* (to make it easier to own). Ex.: a 2-for-1 split — a holder of a $100 share of stock has two $50 shares after the split.

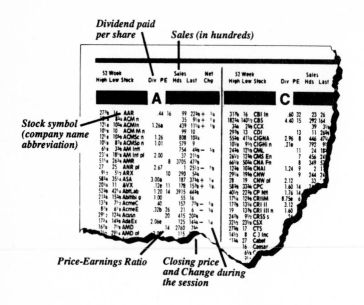

Dividend paid per share

Sales (in hundreds)

Stock symbol (company name abbreviation)

Price-Earnings Ratio

Closing price and Change during the session

What all the little letters mean

Stock Symbol

The name of a publicly-traded company, abbreviated for convenience in financial quotation reporting — in the newspaper financial pages, on wire services, etc. In the newspapers, for example, Hewlett/Packard is *HewlPk*. Also called *ticker symbol*.

STOCK KEY

Sales figures are unofficial. **s** —stock split or stock dividend amounting to 25 percent or more in the past 52 weeks. Dividend begins with the date of split or stock dividend. **n**—new issue in past 52 weeks. **g**—dividend or earnings in Canadian money. Stock trades in U.S. dollars. No yield or PE shown unless stated in U.S. money. Unless otherwise noted, rates of dividends are annual disbursements based on last quarterly or semiannual declaration. Special or extra dividends or payments not designated as regular are identified as follows:

a—also extra or extras. **b**—annual rate plus stock dividend. **c**—liquidating dividend. **e**—declared or paid in preceding 12 months. **i**—declared or paid after stock dividend or split up. **j**—paid this year, dividend omitted, deferred or no action taken at last dividend meeting. **k**—declared or paid this year, an accumulative issue with dividends in arrears **r**—declared or paid in preceding 12 months plus stock dividend. **t**—paid in stock in preceding 12 months, estimated cash value on ex-dividend or ex-distribution date.

x—ex-dividend or ex-rights. **y**—ex-dividend and sales in full. **z**—sales in full.

cld—called. **wd**—when distributed. **wi**—when issued. **ww**—with warrants. **xw**—without warrants. **xdis**—ex-distribution.

vi—in bankruptcy or receivership or being reorganized under bankruptcy act, or securities assumed by such companies.

Stop-Loss

Designed to prevent continued loss; a customer's standing order to his broker to sell a stock or a commodity contract if the price drops to a certain point.

Stop Order

The order from a customer to a broker to sell at the *stop price* (activates a stop order).

....

(The) Story

The pitch (by a corporate management, broker, etc.) that makes a stock irresistible.

....

Straddle

A put and a call option combined, *both* for the same security or commodity, at the same price, for the same period. The options are usually purchased together, but may be sold separately, to hedge risk. See also: HEDGING, OPTION

....

Straight-Line Depreciation   See: DEPRECIATION
Strategic Metals   See: METALS

....

Strategy

A plan, method or series of maneuvers to obtain a specific result; ex.: a commodity trading strategy.

....

Strike   See: UNION
Subchapter S   See: BUSINESS STRUCTURES
Sublease   See: LEASE

....

Supply & Demand

Economic Theory: Price is a function of supply and demand; when demand is greater than supply, prices go up, but if supply outstrips demand, prices fall. Simple.

....

Subsidy

Direct governmental financial aid given to a farm(er), a private industrial group, a charity, etc. A *grant* or contribution of money. *Subsidize:* giving a subsidy.

> ***"When a fellow says, 'It ain't the money but the principle of the thing,' it's the money."***
> *Frank McKinney Hubbard*

Summary Judgement

Law: A judgement, as in a debt action that is entered without a jury trial, after creditor and debtor affidavits convince the court there is no arguable issue.

Superagency

A very large agency; esp. a big government agency that oversees smaller agencies.

Supply-Side

Economics: A theory holding that reducing taxes (particularly for businesses and higher bracket individuals) encourages business investment and growth. This presumably stimulates and stabilizes the economy, and in the long-term brings higher tax revenues on the increased activity.
See also: TRICKLE-DOWN

Supply-Sider

One who advocates supply-side economics (usually an economist or a politician).

....

Support Level (Price)

The price below which a company's stock is not supposed to drop, because of the company's actual asset worth.

Support Price

Price at which the government will buy commodities to maintain a certain price level. Also: *support level* — usually refers to agricultural products. See also: SUBSIDY

....

Surety

A pledge, guaranty or bond. Security against loss or damage or for the fulfillment of an obligation, the payment of a debt, etc.

....

Surplus

An amount greater than needed. Ex.: a nation's agricultural produce in excess of its needs, esp. if purchased and stored by the government to guarantee farmers a specific (*support*) price.

....

Surrender   See: INSURANCE

Surtax   See: TAX

....

Survivor

Law: One of two or more designated persons (such as *joint tenants* or others having a joint interest) who outlives the other(s).

Survivorship

The rights of a person to property on the death of another having joint interest. If more than two joint tenants, the property passes to successive survivors. Also called the *rights of survivorship*.

Sweep Account

A checking account from which money (in excess of a specified amount) is automatically transferred to another account that earns a higher rate of return.

Swiss Banking   See: GNOMES OF ZURICH, NUMBERED ACCOUNT

Syndicate (-ation)

Banking, Real Estate: A group of bankers or capitalists formed to carry out a project requiring large capital resources. Ex.: the underwriting of an issue of stock or a large construction project, etc.

"Money is a terrible master but an excellent servant."
P.T. Barnum

Takeaway

Employee benefits eliminated or reduced by a union contract's terms. Also called a *takeback*.

....

Take-Home (Pay)

Money left from a salary or wage check *after* deductions: withholding taxes, Social Security, etc.

....

Takeover

Acquiring ownership or control of a corporation by stock purchase or exchange. (The corporation is a *takeover target*.) A *hostile takeover* is attempted by parties unacceptable to the corporation's shareholders and existing management; a *friendly takeover* is by an acceptable party.

Corporate Raider

A group or person who attempts an unfriendly takeover. Also called a *predator*.

LBO

Abbr.: **Leveraged Buy-Out.** Using borrowed funds to take over a company. Assets of the company being bought may serve as collateral for loans to make the purchase; the loans are then paid off out of cash flow or by selling off some of the company's assets. (A corporation's management may use this technique to take a public company private, to avoid hostile takeover.)

Poison Pill

A device used by a company to avoid takeover. Ex.: selling off part of the business, or issuing a new class of stock that favors existing stockholders and makes it more (too) costly for a would-be raider. Also called a *porcupine provision* or *shark repellant*.

White Knight

A (friendly) company that rescues a target company from (hostile) takeover.

....

Tariff

The official list of a government's (customs) duties on imports or exports. Also: a *duty* or *rate* on the list.

....

▶ Tax

Money demanded by a government for its support or for specific services, levied on income, property, sales, etc. Also: the *act of taxing. Taxable income:* income, after deductions, subject to tax. *Taxpayer:* a person who pays or is subject to a tax. *Tax rate:* the percentage of income or property value on which tax is paid.

> *"Every child born in America can hope to grow up to enjoy tax loopholes."*
> **TRB (Richard Stout)**

● **Direct Tax**

Tax taken directly from the obligated person, not collected by a second party; ex.: property tax.

Assess

Placing value on real or personal property by a taxing authority for the purpose of taxation. *Assessment:* Amount assessed, particularly for a special purpose such as road or sewer improvement that also improves the property. The *assessor* is the one who sets valuations — assesses. *Assessed valuation* is the value assessed, usually a percentage of actual value; tax is a number of dollars per thousand dollars of valuation.

> *"Capital punishment: income tax."*
> **Jeff Hayes**

Capital Gains Tax

Tax on gains on invested capital.

Estimated Tax

Tax prepaid on expected income.

Gift Tax

Tax on gifts of more than $10,000 value.

> **"The only thing that hurts
> more than paying an income tax
> is not having to pay an income tax."**
> *Lord Thomas R. Duwar*

GRANT

Income Tax
National, state and/or city governments' tax on individual and business income.

Progressive Tax
A system in which higher incomes are taxed at a higher percentage rate than are lower incomes. Also called a *graduated tax*.

A *flat tax* is applied at the same rate to all income levels.

Regressive Tax is the opposite of progressive tax: the rate drops as the tax base increases (which results in lower incomes being taxed at higher rates).

Withholding Tax
Income tax withheld by an employer from an employee's wages and paid directly to the government. *Payroll tax deduction:* Federal, state, city taxes on workers' wages, withheld by the employer. (Reported on IRS W-2 and appropriate local forms.)

Pretax
Before tax is paid. Ex.: pretax income.

Property Tax
Tax levied on real or personal property.

Sales Tax

Tax on receipts from sales, which is added to the selling price.

● Indirect Tax

Tax included in the price of goods, which the consumer pays indirectly — perhaps, unknowingly. Also called *hidden tax*.

> **"Why does a slight tax increase cost you two hundred dollars and a substantial tax cut save you thirty cents?"**
> *Peg Bracken*

Estate Tax

Imposed on inherited property, assessed on the estate's gross value prior to distribution to the heirs. Also called *death tax* or *inheritance tax*.

Excise Tax

Internal, i.e., within a country; tax on certain commodities (liquor, tobacco, etc.), levied on manufacture, sale or consumption. Also called a *use tax*; the one actually using or consuming the product pays the tax.

Franchise Tax

A territorial (usually a state) tax.

Luxury Tax

On goods (usually expensive) considered non-essential.

Stamp Tax

Revenue comes from the sale of stamps required on certain merchandise or legal documents. *Tax stamp*: the stamp affixed to indicate tax is paid.

Surtax

An add-on tax; additional tax on something already taxed — maybe even on a tax. Usually for a specific purpose.

VAT

Abbr.: **Value-Added Tax**. A tax based on value added to a product at each stage of production. Ex.: with product parts for assembly into a finished product, the difference between the parts' original value and their assembled value is taxed as value added. Also called *TVA in Europe* — tax on value added.

Tax Accountant

Accountant specialized in tax procedure and law. Also a *tax advisor* or *tax consultant* (not necessarily an accountant).

> *"Nothing makes a man and wife feel closer, these days, than a joint tax return."*
> **Gil Stern**

Tax Bracket

The tax rate applied to taxable income within a certain range (between brackets) on the tax schedules. The higher the bracket, the more the tax. *Bracket creep* is gradual upward movement into a higher tax bracket.

> *"I'm proud to be paying taxes*
> *in the United States.*
> *The only thing is—I could be*
> *just as proud for half the money."*
> Arthur Godfrey

Tax Credit

A reduction of tax due allowed to the taxpayer by the taxing body.

Tax Deduction

An expenditure that is *deductible*, reduces taxable income; ex.: charitable contributions are deductible.

Tax Deferred

Income not taxed until a later time; ex.: an IRA.

Tax Evasion

Nonpayment of taxes; ex.: failure to report, or inaccurate reporting of taxable income.

Tax Exempt

Not subject to taxation — ever; released from tax obligation. Ex.: tax exempt municipal bonds. Also called *tax-free*.

Exemption

Taxpayer's circumstances or status — dependents, age, etc. — that qualify as allowable deductions from his/her taxable income.

Tax Haven

A foreign country used for a residence or a foreign corporation used for doing business, in order to avoid or reduce income taxes in one's home country.

Tax Return

Income result reported (on government forms). Also the *form*; IRS form 1040 for individuals.

Tax Shelter

Financial arrangements (certain investments, allowances, etc.) that reduce or eliminate taxes due. Such income is *tax sheltered* (a red flag to the IRS).

> *"Taxes are going up so fast that government is likely to price itself right out of the market."*
>   Dan Bennett

Technical Analysis
    See: INVESTMENT ANALYST
Telephone Switch
    See: MUTUAL FUND
Tenant   See: RENT

Tenancy in Common

A person's share of a property (owned by two or more parties) which automatically passes to his estate on his death, and not to the other surviving owners. See also JOINT TENANCY

Tender (Offer)

A written offer to do work, supply something, etc., at a given cost: a bid. A *formal offer,* presented formally.

Tenement   See: REAL ESTATE
Term Life Insurance   See: INSURANCE
Theft Insurance   See: INSURANCE
Third Party Insurance   See: INSURANCE

....

Third World
Underdeveloped nations, esp. the poorer ones.

....

Ticker (tape)
Obsolete: a telegraphic receiver that automatically printed out market prices and data received from financial reporting services on a paper tape. Today, this is an electronic service. A *ticker symbol* is the same as a stock symbol.

....

Time Deposit
A deposit that can be withdrawn by the depositor only after an agreed time has elapsed; longer time deposits normally earn higher interest rates. There are penalties for early withdrawal.   See also CD

....

Time Money
Money loaned to be repaid within a specified period of time, usually in installments.

....

Time Note
A note payable within a specified time after it is presented.

....

Timeshare   See: REAL ESTATE

....

Tip

To provide private or secret (financial) information.
A *tipster* furnishes tips.

Titanium   See: STRATEGIC METALS

Title

Real Estate: Legal right to the possession of a property.

Abstract of Title

The history of a property summarizing all related
transactions — transfer by deed and will, previous
owners, lienholders, etc. It's brought up-to-date each
time the property changes ownership.

Just Title

A correct title; also called a *clear title*.

Title Company

A company that does title work, updating, etc., and
makes sure a title is clear. The company is liable for
the accuracy of its work.

Title Deed

A document containing evidence of ownership.

Title Insurance

Insurance protecting an owner, mortgagee, or property
from lawsuits or claims due to a defective title.

Toll

A fee extracted by state or local authorities for some
privilege — use of a road, a bridge, etc. A tax or duty.
Toll-free: without toll.

> *"That money talks*
> *I'll not deny,*
> *I heard it once,*
> *it said, 'Goodbye.' "*
> *Richard Armor*

Tort

A wrongful act (excluding breach of contract or trust) that results in injury to another's person, property, reputation, etc., and which entitles the injured to compensation.

Tout

Soliciting business, employment, votes, etc., in an annoying manner.

Townhouse   See: REAL ESTATE

Trade

Buying, selling or exchanging wholesale or retail commodities, in one country or between countries. A purchase or sale, business deal or transaction. Also called *traffic*.

Trade Association

Individuals or companies in a specific business, organized to promote common interests.

Trade Balance   See: BALANCE OF TRADE

Trade Barrier

A regulation that restricts international trade: a tariff or quota. See also EMBARGO

Trade Deficit/Surplus   See: BALANCE OF TRADE

Trade Discount

A discount on the price of goods given by the manufacturer or wholesaler to a retailer. Often related to the volume purchased.

Trader

One who trades — merchant, businessperson, broker. Also: a *stock exchange member* trading privately, but not for customers. See also BARTER, BROKER, COMMODITIES

Trading Floor (Station, Desk)

Locations within a national stock exchange where trading takes place.

Trading Range

Commodities: The maximum set limit which a commodity price is allowed to move during a trading session.

Securities: The range within which a security has traded during a trading session (there are no set limits).

Trading Session (Day)

The period during a 24-hour day when trading takes place on an exchange. (*Note:* because of the worldwide nature of today's markets and modern transaction processing technology, it's expected trading will soon be non-stop, 24-hours a day.)

Trading Unit

The quantity of one security that can be traded on an exchange (100 shares, 5000 lbs., etc.).

Trading Volume

The amount of a security or group of securities traded during a specific time period.

....

Trade Union See: UNION

....

Transact

To carry on or conduct (business, negotiations, activities, etc.) to a conclusion or settlement. *Transaction*: something transacted, esp. a business agreement.

....

Transfer Agent

A person, bank or trust company that acts officially for a corporation to execute and record its stock transfers from one legal owner to another.

....

Transportations   See: DOW-JONES
....

Travelers' Check

A check issued (in various denominations) by a bank, travel agency, etc., signed by the purchaser upon purchase, and signed again — witnessed by the payee — when the check is cashed.

....

Treasury (Department of)

Department of government that has control over collection, management and disbursement of public revenue.

The country's bank account

U.S. TREASURY

(Figures in millions)

Total public debt Nov. 21	2,635,224
Statutory debt limit	2,800,000
Operating balance Nov. 21	14,364
Interest fiscal 1989 thru Oct.	15,157
Interest period fiscal 1988	14,115
Estimated deficit fiscal 1989	145,500
Actual deficit fiscal 1988	155,102
Receipts fiscal 1989 thru Oct.	63,646
Receipts period fiscal 1988	62,354
Outlays fiscal 1989 thru Oct.	91,086
Outlays period fiscal 1988	93,164
Gold assets thru Sept.	11,062

▶ Treasuries

Bills, bonds, notes, etc., securities sold by the government when borrowing is necessary to raise revenues. Treasuries' rates are watched carefully by the private banking and investment communities as guides to the government's policies and direction interest and inflation rates are headed.

● **Savings Bond**

　　U.S. government bond in amounts up to $10,000.

● **Treasury Bill (T-Bill)**

　　Government promissory notes in denominations from
　　$1,000 to $1,000,000, with maturities of less than a
　　year. T-Bills pay no interest, but are sold at a discount.

● **Treasury Bond (T-Bond)**

　　Any of the interest-bearing bonds issued by the
　　Treasury, with maturities of 10-years or longer.

● **Treasury Certificate**

　　Government obligations — $1000 to $1,000,000 —
　　represented by certificates maturing in one year or less,
　　with interest periodically paid on the redemption of
　　coupons. Treasury certificates are like bank CDs (the
　　interest rate paid is usually slightly higher) and are
　　the most familiar and popular of the Treasury's public
　　offerings. Treasury certificates are often mistakenly
　　referred to as T-Bills.

● **T-Note**

　　Treasury note; up to 10-years maturity, pays interest
　　semi-annually.

*Many financial pages also report corporate bonds. Though it gets less publicity,
the bond market raises more money than does the stock market.*

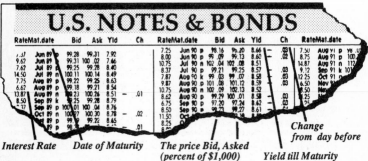

U.S. NOTES & BONDS

Interest Rate　　Date of Maturity　　The price Bid, Asked　　Yield till Maturity　　Change from day before
(percent of $1,000)

> **"Those who condemn wealth
> are those who have none and
> see no chance of getting it."**
> *William Penn Patrick*

Trickle-Down (Theory)

The idea that government policies (tax, spending, etc.) that benefit big business and wealthy individuals, stimulate the economy and eventually *trickle-down* to the benefit of communities and less wealthy individuals. See also REAGANOMICS, SUPPLY-SIDE ECONOMICS

Truck Farm See: REAL ESTATE

Trust

Law: A fiduciary relationship in which one person (the *trustee*) holds the title to property (the *trust estate* or *trust property*) for the benefit of another (the *beneficiary*). Also: the *property* so-held.

Trust Account

An account of property one establishes with a *trust company* for distribution per the terms of the trust creating the account.

Trust Company

A company set up to exercise the functions of a *trustee*. (Usually also engages in other financial activities.)

Trustee

A person — usually one of several — appointed to administer the affairs of a company, institution, etc. Also a person who holds the title to property for the benefit of another.

Trustee in Bankruptcy

One appointed by a court to administer the property of another who is bankrupt.

Trust Fund

Money, securities, property, etc., held in trust.

Monopoly: An illegal combination of companies — a *trust* — in which one board of trustees controls the member companies' stock. This makes it possible to manage the combine to minimize production costs, control prices, eliminate competition, etc. Also any large company or combine that has *monopolistic control* over the production of a commodity or service. See also ANTI-TRUST, MONOPOLY

Truth in Advertising

Legal requirement for advertisements, labels, etc., to contain complete and truthful information, in order to honestly represent products to the consumer.

Truth in Lending

Legal requirement for lenders to disclose and explain all charges and terms to their borrowers.

Umbrella Policy   See: INSURANCE

....

Unbundled Stock (Unit)

Abbr.: **USU.** An anti-takeover device that is one-part debt
and two-parts equity: a bond, a preferred share and a redeemable equity appreciation certificate. The unit has no
voting rights and is exchanged for one share of common
stock. A relatively recent product, USU popularity is yet to
be proven.

....

Unconditional

Without conditions; ex.: unconditional guaranty.

....

Underbooked

Potential buyers of a new stock issue indicate limited
interest: the opposite of *fully booked.*

....

Underinsure

To insure a property for an amount less than its actual value or replacement value.

....

Underprice

Pricing goods below cost in order to undercut the competition.

> **"Work is the price you pay for money."**
> *Anonymous*

Undervalued

Valued below real worth; ex.: a stock selling for less than its equity value.

....

Underwrite

Finance: To guarantee sale of securities offered to the public.

Insurance: To accept liability for losses covered by a policy.

Underwriter

A company that underwrites; ex.: an insurance company. Also may be the *person* within such a company with the authority to make the decision to underwrite.

....

Unearned Income

Income from anything but work: property, interest, etc.

....

Unemployment

The state of being out of work.

Unemployment Benefit

Money paid by government, unions, etc. to an (former) employee who is out of work. Also called *unemployment compensation*. *Unemployment insurance* is government insurance that provides these benefits for those eligible.

Unemployment Rate

Number of employable people who are out of work at a given time, stated as a percentage of the employable total.

....

Union

An organization of workers, joined for mutual benefit. *Labor union:* An association of (wage-earning) workers organized to promote and protect the membership's interests through collective bargaining with management. *Trade Union:* A labor union of craftspeople or workers in related crafts, as distinguished from a union including all workers in an industry.

AFL/CIO

Abbr.: **American Federation of Labor and Congress of Industrial Organizations.** A major U.S. labor union. Until their merger in 1955, the AFL and CIO were separate rival organizations.

Closed Shop (Open Shop)

A factory, store, etc. where only union employees may be hired. Also called a *union shop*. *Open shop*: a factory, etc. where both union *and* non-union workers are employed, although a union may act as *bargaining agent* for all. The *right-to-work* is the right of workers to gain or keep employment, whether or not they are union members.

Labor Strike
Refusal by employees to work, in the attempt to gain concessions from their employer. *On strike:* a work stoppage. *Strike benefits:* money paid by a union to strikers in order for them to subsist during a strike. Also called *strike pay.* A *striker* is a person on strike. *Sympathy strike:* a workers' strike, not because of grievances against their own employer, but in support of other workers on strike or locked out. *Wildcat strike:* a workers' strike not authorized by their union. *Strikebound:* closed by a strike; ex.: a strikebound factory. *Strikebreaker:* a person who takes part in breaking up a workers' strike, either by working in the striking workers' place, or by furnishing other workers to do so. Also called a *scab.* A *lockout* is the closing of a business and the employer's refusal to let employees work until they agree to his terms.

Unit Price
The rate, or cost, of something with all extra incidental costs (overhead, etc.) included.

Unload(ing)
To get rid of, dump; ex.: unloading a poorly performing stock.

Unpaid Dividend
A dividend declared that has not yet reached payment date.

Upturn
An upswing of business activity, prices, sales, etc.

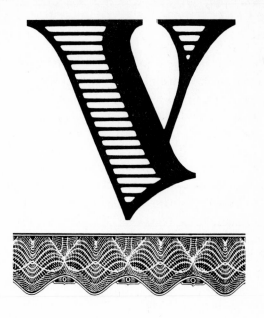

Variable Annuity   See: INSURANCE
Variable Rate   See: INTEREST
VAT   See: TAX

....

Venture Capital

Funds invested or speculated in a new and/or unproven
business (some call it *ad*venture capital). Also called
risk capital. *Venture capitalist:* A person who furnishes
such capital.

....

Vertical Mobility

Moving up to a higher social status: *upward mobility;*
and, of course, there's also *downward* mobility.

....

Vested

Ownership, protected or established by law; ex.: of a
pension plan. See also: RETIREMENT PLAN

....

Void

Not legally binding. Also: to *cancel*.

....

Volatility

Fluctuating sharply; ex.: price or market volatility.

....

Volume

Stock: Shares traded during a trading session.

*"Dividend:
Hush money
to shareholders."*
Jim Fisk & Robert Barron

W-2, W-4, etc.   See: TAX

....

Waiver

Intentionally giving up a right or interest. Also a *written statement* to that effect.

Waiver of Premium   See: INSURANCE

....

Wall Street

NYC street (actually an area) that's the financial center of the U.S. Also called *The Street*.

....

Warrant

A long-term option sold with a preferred stock or bond purchase that entitles the buyer to buy an additional amount of common stock at a set price for a period of time in the future. Also called a *subscription warrant*. See also: OPTIONS

Warranty

A written guarantee given to a new product purchaser by the manufacturer or dealer, that specifies free-of-charge repair and/or replacement of defective parts for a stated period of time (after purchase). A *full warranty* covers the entire product, assuring that if defective, it will be repaired or replaced at no cost. A *limited warranty* specifies what is and is not covered by the warranty. Ex.: parts may be covered, but not labor.

Welfare

Funds provided by government to help needy people, esp. those who can't work.

White Knight   See: TAKEOVER
Whole Life Insurance   See: INSURANCE

Wholesale

Sale of goods in quantity (to retailers, jobbers) for resale.

Will

A legal statement of a person's wishes concerning the disposal of his possessions and property after his death. Also a *document* expressing this wish.

A *living will* is a written statement of one's wishes in the event of a terminal illness, in order to avoid futile treatments.

Workforce
   The total of people available for work.

....

Working Capital
   Capital (cash) needed for a business' day-to-day affairs.

....

Wraparound Mortgage   See: MORTGAGE

> *"In God we trust—all others pay cash."*
> *Sign in an Arkansas Diner*

Write-off
   An uncollectible account cancelled from the books as a loss. Also: *depreciation, reducing book value.*

Write-Down
   A book reduction of an asset (to depreciate the asset).

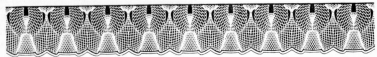

Yield

> To produce (profit). Income from a financial investment, usually stated as a percentage of cost.

Zero-Coupon Bond   See: BOND

Zoned   See: REAL ESTATE

&
THEN
THERE'S...

MONEY slang

Here's a sample of money slang expressions (there are many more). Definitions shown relate to money, but there may be other meanings as well. The expressions often have ethnic, racial, regional or group — carnival, hobo, military, underworld, etc. — origins. Many originated during the Great Depression and are now obsolete.

Abe's Cabe = a five dollar bill.   **Ace** = a one dollar bill.
Angel = one who donates, finances.

Bail Out = to help one who has met with (financial) difficulty.   **Bankroll** = to finance (a project).
Bat Hides = paper money.   **Beewy** = money, coins, change.
Bent = without much money, almost broke.   **Big Boy** or **Big Bill** = $100 (bill).
Big George= a quarter.   **Big One** = $1000 (bill).   **Bite** = expense, cost; (put the bite on) ask for money.   **Black Ink** = profit.   **Bone**= a (silver) dollar.
Boodle = bribe money; taken from public funds — graft.   **Bread** = money.
Buck = $1. (**Half-buck** = 50 cents.)   **In the Bucks** = having money.   **Bundle** = a large amount of money.

C. = $100.   **C. Note, Century** = $100 bill.   **Case Note** = $1 (bill).   **Clam** = $1.   **Cash In** = (one's chips) = end a transaction.   **Cash In On** = to gain a profit or advantage.   **Cats and Dogs** = speculative, low-priced stocks — of (perhaps) marginal value.   **Chips (in the)** = affluent, having money.   **Clip** = cheat, swindle.   **Coin** = money.   **Cream** = easy money.   **Cuff (on the)** = credit (to buy on).

Darby; Dough; Doodle-E-Squat = money.   **Dews** = $10.   **Dime Note; Dix** = $10 bill.   **Double Sawbuck** = $20 (bill).

Eagle Day = payday.   **Easy Street** = financial independence.

Fairy Godfather = financial backer.   **Fast Buck** = easily acquired money.
Fish = $1.   **Frogskin** = $1 bill.   **Fistful (of money)**= large amount; wealth.
Five; Five-Case Note; Five Spot = $5 (bill).   **Flat, Flat Broke** = without money.   **Flyer** = a chance; a gamble.   **Four Bits** = 50 cents (**Two Bits** = 25 cents; **Six Bits** = 75 cents).   **Freebie** = free of charge.

G.I.; Grand = $1000.   **Geets** = money; dollars; buying power.   **Gnomes of Zurich*** = Swiss banking community.   **Gold Digger** = one who associates with another purely for financial gain.   **Graft** = bribery.   **Gravy** = more money than expected; easily gained money.
Gravy Ride = one takes it on the **Gravy Train** = excessive pay for little (no) work; prosperity.   **Grease** = bribe; protection money.   **Green Folding; Green Money; Green Stuff** = money in bills.

Handsome Ransom = much money.   **Happy Money** = money earned or spent for personal enjoyment.   **Hard Money** = money difficult to earn (or borrow).   **Hard Sell** = aggressive, often unpleasant sales or advertising techniques.   **Have-Not** = a poor person, group, nation.   **Hardball** = commodity trading.   **Hay** = small amount of money; **That Ain't Hay** = large amount of money.   **Heavy Hitter** = a very influential or important person.   **Heavy Money (Dough, Jack, Sugar)** = much (influential) money.   **High Roller** = one who spends (invests, speculates) large amounts.

Hit (Someone) = to borrow money; ask for a raise.   **Hock (In); Hole (In The)** = in debt.   **Home Run** = a winning stock, action, etc.   **Hot** = free of charge.   **Hustle** = to sell something— aggressively, perhaps unethically.

Ice = a diamond(s); also a bribe or illegal profit.   **I.O.U.*** = I owe you: a promissory note.   **Iron Man** = a silver dollar.

Jack = money.   **Jack Up** = increase price.   **Jawbone** = to lend, to trust; to borrow, buy on credit.   **Jelly** = anything obtained free of charge.   **Jit** = a nickel, 5 cents; cheap.   **John Hancock (John Henry)** = one's signature.

Kale = money.   **Kickback** = money unethically returned (by a seller) to gain advantage or favors.   **Kick In** = contribute (money).   **Kitty** = a pool of money; total available.   **Knockdown** = to keep money received or collected for one's employer; esp. from a cash register.

Lame Duck = market speculator who bought stock he can't afford.   **Lay Paper** = to cash worthless checks or counterfeit money.   **Leather** = a wallet, pocketbook, purse.   **Leech** = to borrow; esp., without intention to repay.   **Legal Beagle (Eagle)** = a lawyer; esp., one particularly aggressive or astute.   **Lettuce** = paper money.   **Light Piece** = a silver coin, esp. a quarter; a small amount of money.   **Line** = the cost of an item, purchase price; **Lay It (Put It) On The Line** = pay money, pay up; take a chance, risk.   **Loanshark** = a person who lends money at excessively high rates of interest; usurer; **Loansharking** = the act.   **Long Green** = paper money, esp. a large amount.   **Loose** = having little money.   **Lug** = to solicit a loan, to borrow.

M., Moola, Moolah = money.   **Mad Money** = money saved for emergency or an impulsive purchase.   **Main-Line** = money; a community's wealthy, socially prominent people.   **Make (It)** = to attain money, fame, success.   **Marker** = promissory note; I.O.U.   **Mega-bucks** = very large sum of money.   **Melted Out** = without funds; broke.   **Michigan Roll** = a genuine bill around a roll of fake bills.   **Midas** = one of great wealth.   **Midas Touch** = ability to turn business ventures into very profitable ones.

Mingy = mean and stingy.   **Miser** = a stingy person.   **(In The) Mom & Pop Shop** = a small retail business — grocery, convenience store, etc.— that may be owned and run by a family.   **Monied** = having money, esp. a lot. **Moneybags** = a wealthy person.   **Moneyman** = an investor, angel, backer; one who manages a business' money.   **Money Player** = one who performs best under competitive pressure.   **Money Talks** = wealth is power.

Nest Egg = money saved, esp. over a long period of time. **Nickel Nurser** = a miser.   **New Money, New Rich** = those possessing wealth recently earned.   **Nut** = total expenses to start or to operate a business; overhead. **(Crack the Nut** = break even.)

Old Money = those who have had wealth a long time. **Oil** = money, esp. graft.   **One-Shot** = a one-time business transaction; one chance.   **On The Make** = ambitious; intent on advancing one's financial position or profit.   **On The Rocks** = without funds.   **Ooftish, Ooks** = money.

Pack It In = to earn or win as much money, fame, etc. as a given(favorable) situation will allow. **Pap** = money.   **Paper** = counterfeit money; passing counterfeit money or bad checks;   **Paper-Hanger (Paper Pusher)** = one who cashes or forges bad checks; **Paper Hanging** = the act.   **Parlay** = to start with a small amount (of money) and increase it.

Pay Dirt = a desired(financial) result; a goal.   **Payola**= graft; blackmail; also a payroll.   **Pay Through The Nose** = pay excessively. **Peanut** = a small business venture; small amount of money, a small profit. **Penny Ante** = involving small sums (of money).   **Penny Pincher** = a stingy or frugal person.   **Piece Of Change (Jack)** = an amount of money.   **Piker** = stingy person; miser.   **Pile** = large sum of money.   **Pinch Gut** = miser. **Plaster** = a bank note, esp. a $1 bill.   **Plastic** = credit card(s).   **Pluck** = to rob, cheat.   **Plum** = very desirable or profitable: a "plum" job.   **Plush (Posh)** = luxurious, chic, expensive.   **Plunk (Plank) Down** = pay money.   **Poison Pill*** = devices used by a company to avoid Takeover.   **Poke** = wallet, purse.   **Pony Up** = to pay.   **Poor Man's** = cheaper version.   **Pot Of Gold** = sudden wealth, a windfall.   **Pull Down** = earn (money).   **Push** = advertise, publicize.

Queer = counterfeit.   **Quick (Fast) Buck** = money easily gained.   **Rain Check** = a promise to honor an offer at a later date.   **Rake Off** = commission, percentage received by a party to a transaction.   **Rat Race** = job, business, etc. in which activity seems more important than results.   **Raw Deal** = an unfair treatment or business transaction.   **Ready (The)** = money, esp. cash.   **Red Ink** = financial deficit, loss.   **Right Money** = smart (application of) money.   **Rip Off** = to cheat, swindle.   **Rubber Check** = one that bounces because of insufficient funds.   **Rust Belt** =industrialized northeastern U.S. where older factories and industries are located.

Sawbuck; Saw = $10 (bill).   **Scandal Sheet** = expense account. **Scissorsbill** = one whose income isn't from wages; a rich person.   **Scratch** = money.   **Script** = $1 (bill); money.   **Single** = $1 (bill).   **Scrounge** = habitual borrower. **Scrounge Up (Around)** = seeking money to borrow.   **Set (Someone) Back** = to cost money.   **Set Up** = to prepare someone to be swindled; also: one easily swindled.   **Shark** = one who preys on others.   **Shell Game** = a swindle or a fraud.   **Shell Out** = to pay, contribute.   **Shill** = a decoy; a hustle.   **Shoe-String** = small amount (of capital).   **Short** = having little (not enough) money.   **Side (On The)** = earn extra money.   **Silver Jeff** = 25 cents (a quarter).   **Silver Wing** = 50 cents (coin).   **Simple Simon** = a diamond.   **Skip**= to leave quickly (without paying bills).   **Skim** = to take the best from (business, profit).   **Slick** = to dupe, cheat.   **Smart Money** = investments in a sure thing.   **Soak** = to charge heavily; overcharge.   **Soap** = money, esp. a bribe.   **Sock** = place where money is kept; a (large) sum of money.   **Soft** = easy money.   **Soft Money** = paper money.   **Soft Sell** = to sell non-aggressively.   **Soft Touch** = one who lends generously, one easily cheated.   **Sow** = 5 cents (a nickel).   **Sparkler** = a diamond, a gem or a ring.   **Sponge** = a moocher; to mooch.   **Square Deal** = fair.   **Squeeze** = graft; a miser.   **Squeezed** = financial trouble.   **Stake** = a sum of money, borrowed or saved, to start a venture; to back someone in a venture.   **Stash** = to save, hide away.   **Stiff, Sting** = to cheat.   **Stone Broke** = having no money at all.   **(On A) Streak (A Roll)** = a run of good fortune.   **Strapped** = broke.   **Sugar** = money; money for pleasure; bribe money.   **Sugar Daddy** = a backer, financier.   **Swag** = money, valuables.

Tab = a bill; an I.O.U.   **Take (The)** = profit; **To Take** = cheat. **Take A Bath** = to lose — on a stock, etc.   **Take A Flier** = take a chance, esp. a long shot.   **Tap Out** = go broke.   **Ten; Ten Spot** = $10 (bill).   **Thin** = broke. **Thin One** = 10 cents (a dime).   **Thou** = $1000.   **Throw Money** = change.   **(On) Tick** = credit.   **Tight (Fisted, Wad)** = tight, stingy.   **Tight Money** = money hard to earn or borrow.   **Top Dollar** = the maximum being or likely to be paid.   **Touch** = ask for a loan.   **Tough Buck** = hard earned.   **Turkey** = a loser, as a turkey stock.   **Turn A Dollar** = earn money.   **Two Spot** = $2 bill.   **Tycoon** = businessperson of great wealth and power.

Under-The-Table (-Counter) = a secret deal, payment —perhaps crooked.

Valentine = notice of dismissal (from a job).   **Velvet** = profit; money. **Vigorish** = interest paid to a loanshark.

Walking Papers = notice of dismissal.   **Wheeler-Dealer** = one with many business affairs; a schemer.   **Widows & Orphans (Securities)** = very conservative investments.   **Wooden Nickel** = a sucker deal.   **Wunderkind** = one who succeeds, esp. in business, esp. a young hotshot.

Yard = $1000 (bill).   **Year** = one dollar (banknote); **Ten Years** = $10, etc.

Zillion = a number larger than can be imagined.

* Defined in the alphabetical listing

SOME OTHER PEOPLE'S
MONEY
DM £ FF SF

Following are samples of some other countries interesting
monetary units that you may not see every day. Note similarities
that probably result from geography or present and past political
associations. Even then, primary or fractional units often vary
from the neighbor's next door. Exchange rates change daily.

	Primary	Fractional
Algeria	*dinar*	centime
Austria	*schilling*	groschen
Bahrain	*dinar*	fils
Bolivia	*peso boliviano*	centavo
Brazil	*cruzeiro*	centavo
Chile	*peso*	centesimo
China	*yuan*	fen
Costa Rica	*colon*	centimo
Czechoslovakia	*koruna*	haler
Denmark	*krone*	øre
Ecuador	*sucre*	centavo
Egypt	*pound*	piaster
El Salvador	*colon*	centavo
Ethiopia	*birr*	cent
Finland	*markka*	penni
Germany, West	*deutsche mark*	pfennig
Greece	*drachma*	lepton
Guatemala	*quetzal*	centavo
Guinea	*syli*	kori
Haiti	*gourde*	centime
Honduras	*lempira*	centavo
Hungary	*forint*	fillér
Iceland	*krōna*	eyrir
India	*rupee*	paisa
Indonesia	*rupiah*	sen
Iran	*rial*	dinar
Ireland	*pound*	penny
Israel	*shekel*	agora

	Primary	Fractional
Japan	*yen*	—
Korea, North	*won*	jeon
Lybia	*dinar*	milleime
Mongolia	*tugrik*	mongo
Morocco	*dirham*	franc
Netherlands	*guilder*	cent
Nigeria	*naira*	kobo
Oman	*rial*	baiza
Panama	*balboa*	centesimo
Paraguay	*guarani*	centimo
Peru	*sol*	centavo
Poland	*ztoty*	grosz
Portugal	*escudo*	centavo
Romania	*leu*	ban
Saudi Arabia	*riyal*	qursh
South Africa	*rand*	cent
Spain	*peseta*	centimo
Thailand	*baht*	satang
USSR	*ruble*	kopeck
Vatican City	*lira*	centesimo
Venezuela	*bolívar*	centimo
Vietnam	*dong*	sau
Western Samoa	*tala*	sene

MONEY MEDIA

Here's a sample of readily available sources for current
personal finance and investment information.*

BARRON'S
Investors' weekly tabloid.

BusinessWeek
Weekly general business magazine.

Forbes
Twice-monthly magazine of business and financial news.

FORTUNE
Monthly business/financial magazine.

Money

Monthly magazine dealing with financial and investment
subjects of interest to the individual.

THE WALL STREET JOURNAL.

5-day a week business/financial/investment tabloid.

Business/financial T.V. program.

Dick Fabian's
Telephone Switch Newsletter

Market Letters: Subscription newsletters are available on nearly any conceivable money subject. From time to time, the business press reports on how well the market letters' recommendations match their actual performance.

AND . . . Many newspapers have excellent finance/business sections, and local and national T.V. and radio stations offer financial news segments and specials. For those who take their money news very seriously, there are even financial news networks. Also, libraries and bookstores offer volumes on every financial subject.

The *Economist* magazine in the U.K. is known for extensive international economic news, while the *Financial Times* is the English counterpart to *The Wall Street Journal.* Most industrialized countries offer comparable media in their national languages. $

Names, logos, trademarks are the properties of the various publishers.

MONEY I.N.I.T.I.A.L.S.

ADR = Automatic Dividend Reinvestment. **AMEX** = American Stock Exchange. **AFL-CIO** = American Federation of Labor/Congress of Industrial Organizations.* **APR** = Annual Percentage Rate.* **AVP** = Assistant Vice President.

BBB = Better Business Bureau.*

CB = Chairman of the Board.*
CD = Certificate of Deposit.*
CEO = Chief Executive Officer. **CFO** = Chief Financial Officer. **COO** = Chief Operating Officer. **CPA** = Certified Public Accountant.* **CPI**= Consumer Price Index. **COMEX** = Commodity Exchange, Inc.

D&B = Dunn and Bradstreet.* **DBA** = Doing Business As . . .* **EPS** = Earnings per Share.* **EEC** = European Economic Community.* **EMS** = European Monetary System.* **ESOP** = Employee Stock Ownership Plan. **EVP** = Executive Vice President.

FDA = Food and Drug Administration. **FDI** = Foreign Direct Investment. **FDIC** = Federal Deposit Insurance Corporation.* **FHLMC** = Federal Home Loan Mortgage Corporation. **FHA** = Federal Housing Association.* **FED** = Federal Reserve System.* **FIFO**= First In, First Out. **FISH** = First In, Still Here. **FNIC** = Financial New Composite Index. **FSLIC** = Federal Savings and Loan Insurance Corporation.* **FTC** = Federal Trade Commission.

GAO = General Accounting Office. **GI** = Gross Income.* **GIGO**= Garbage In, Garbage Out. **GNP** = Gross National Product.*

HMO = Health Maintenance Organization.*

IMF = International Monetary Fund.*
IPO = Initial Public Offer (of stock).*
IRA = Individual Retirement Account.*
IRS = Internal Revenue Service.*

KBOT = Kansas City Board of Trade.
KEOGH = a tax deferred retirement plan.*

LMM = Liquid Money Market. **LIFO** = Last In, First Out.

NASDAQ = National Association of Securities Dealers Quotation System.   **NTCTE** = New York Cotton Exchange.   **NYF** = New York Futures Exchange.   **NYME** = New York Mercantile Exchange.

OBO = Order Book Official.   **OPEC** = Organization of Petroleum Exporting Countries.   **OSHA** = Occupational Safety and Health Act. **OTC** = Over The Counter.*

PAC = Political Action Committee.   **PIK** = Payment in Kind.*   **P&L** = Profit and Loss.*   **P/E** = Price to Earnings (ratio).*   **PLAM** = Price Level Adjusted Mortgage.*   **PPI** =Producer's Price Index.
PSE = Pacific Stock Exchange.

R&D = Research and Development.
REIT = Real Estate Investment Trust.
RELP =Real Estate Limited Partnership.

S&H = Shipping and Handling.   **S&L** = Savings and Loan.*   **SBA** = Small Business Administration.*   **SBIC** = Small Business Insurance Company. **SBLI** = Savings Bank Life Insurance. **SEC** = Securities and Exchange Commission.   **SEPP** = Simplified Employee Pension Plan.*   **SIP** = Supplemental Income Plan.   **SLIC** = Savings and Loan Insurance Corporation.* **SSA** = Social Security Administration.

TVA = Value Added Tax. (In the **EEC**. Same as **VAT**.)

USPO (**USPS**) = U.S. Post Office (Service).   **USU** = Unbundled Stock Unit.

VAT = Value Added Tax.*   **VP** = Vice President.   **VRM** = Variable Rate Mortgage.*

* Defined in the alphabetical listing.

EXTREMES:

> *"Greed . . . is good."*
> *from the film*
> **Wall Street**

> *"The love of money is the root of all evil."*
> **The Bible**

???

Acknowledgements

The Money Manual draws on a number of references. For more information, the reader is referred to these excellent sources: *The Random House Dictionary of the English Language, 2nd. ed. unabridged* , from Random House; *Webster's New World Dictionary* (2nd ed.), from World Publishing; *Webster's New World Dictionary of Business Terms*, by William Cook, from Simon & Schuster; *Barron's Dictionary of Finance and Investment Terms*, by John Downes and Jordan Elliot Goodman, from Barron's Financial Series; *The World Book Encyclopedia*, by Field Enterprises; *The Wall Street Journal — Guide to Understanding Money & Markets*, by Richard Saul Wurman, Alan Siegel & Kenneth M. Morris, from Access Press (Simon & Schuster); *How to Read the Financial Pages*, by Peter Passell, from Warner Books; *The A to Z of Investing* by Christine Ammer, from Mentor (New American Library); *Wall Street Words*, by David L. Scott, from Houghton Mifflin; *The Zurich Axioms* , by Max Gunther, from Signet; *One Up on Wall Street*, by Peter Lynch, from Simon & Schuster; *ABZs of Money & Finance,* by Susan Lee, from Poseidon Press (Simon & Schuster); *Familiar Quotations,* by John Bartlett, from Little, Brown; *A New Dictionary of Quotations,* by H. L. Mencken, from Knopf (Random House); *The Official MBA Handbook of Great Business Quotations,* selected by Jim Fisk and Robert Barron, from Fireside (Simon & Schuster); *The Pocket Dictionary of American Slang,* by Harold Wentworth and Stuart Berg Flexner, from Pocket Books (Simon & Schuster); *Peter's Quotations* by Dr. Laurence J. Peter, from Bantam (William Morrow & Co.); *The Wall Street Journal* and the business pages of the *San Francisco Chronicle*; *Money* and *Forbes* magazines; brochures and prospectuses from *Fidelity Mutual Funds*.

Data gathered was written and edited for the layman, then checked by editors, proofreaders, and money professionals for correctness and accuracy. The professionals: Leon M. Blum, financial planner; Elliot Buchdrucker, C.P.A.; Stephen Clarke, investment and retirement consultant; L.W. Jacobs, III, banker; Kenneth James, C.P.A. & tax consultant; Robert C. Kahn, insurance broker; Andrea Reed, C.P.A.; George Young, editorial consultant.

To all: appreciation, gratitude, a thousand thanks.

215

About the Author

Bill McKee got through
the University of Missouri
by working for a printer
— which was also where
he learned advertising.
Next came a stint as an
art director, another as
a creative director, and
finally one as a European
ad agency manager. Only
to find his loves are words
and pictures — which
he now freelances from
Bolinas, CA. From the
same house he shares
with wife Arlene. And
two Yorkies.

Credits

Editor
Lloyd Kahn, Jr.

Design & Illustration
Bill McKee

Production Editor
Michael Rafferty

Typesetters
Joan Creed
Michael Rafferty

Proofreading
Sara Safdie

Printing
R.R. Donnelley & Sons, Inc.
Crawfordsville, Indiana

Photostats
Marinstat
Mill Valley, California

Typeface
Times

Book Paper
60 lb. Pentair Suede

Typesetting
Macintosh II CX,
Microsoft Word
Aldus Pagemaker 3.0

Final Copy
Linotronic 300
Postscript RIP #3
Desktop Publishing
San Rafael, California

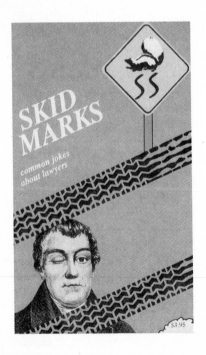